CREATIVE PROJECTS

Quick and Easy Art Projects

by Denise Bieniek, M.S.
Illustrated by Marilyn Mets

10 9 8 7 6 5 4 3

🌐💡 **Troll**✏️
CREATIVE
▲▲▲▲▲▲▲▲▲▲▲▲▲▲▲
TEACHER
IDEAS

Troll Creative Teacher Ideas was designed to help today's dedicated, time-pressured teacher. Created by teachers for teachers, this innovative series provides a wealth of classroom ideas to help reinforce important concepts and stimulate your students' creative thinking skills.

Each book in the series focuses on a different curriculum theme to give you the flexibility to teach any given skill at any time of the year. The wide range of ideas and activities included in each book are certain to help you create an atmosphere where students are continually eager to learn new concepts and develop important skills.

We hope this comprehensive series will provide you with everything you need to foster a fun and challenging learning environment for your students. **Troll Creative Teacher Ideas** is a resource you'll turn to again and again!

Titles in this series:

Classroom Decor:
Decorate Your Classroom from Bulletin Boards to Time Lines

Creative Projects: Quick and Easy Art Projects

Earth Alert: Environmental Studies for Grades 4-6

Explore the World: Social Studies Projects and Activities

Healthy Bodies, Healthy Minds

Holidays Around the World: Multicultural Projects and Activities

It All Adds Up: Math Skill-Building Activities for Grades 4-6

Learning Through Literature:
Projects and Activities for Linking Literature and Writing

Story Writing: Creative Writing Projects and Activities

Think About It: Skill-Building Puzzles Across the Curriculum

The World Around Us: Geography Projects and Activities

World Explorers: Discover the Past

Metric Conversion Chart

1 inch = 2.54 cm	1 foot = .305 m	1 yard = .914 m
1 mile = 1.61 km	1 fluid ounce = 29.573 ml	1 cup = .24 l
1 pint = .473 l	1 teaspoon = 4.93 ml	1 tablespoon = 14.78 ml

Contents

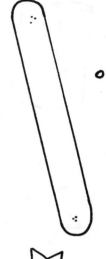

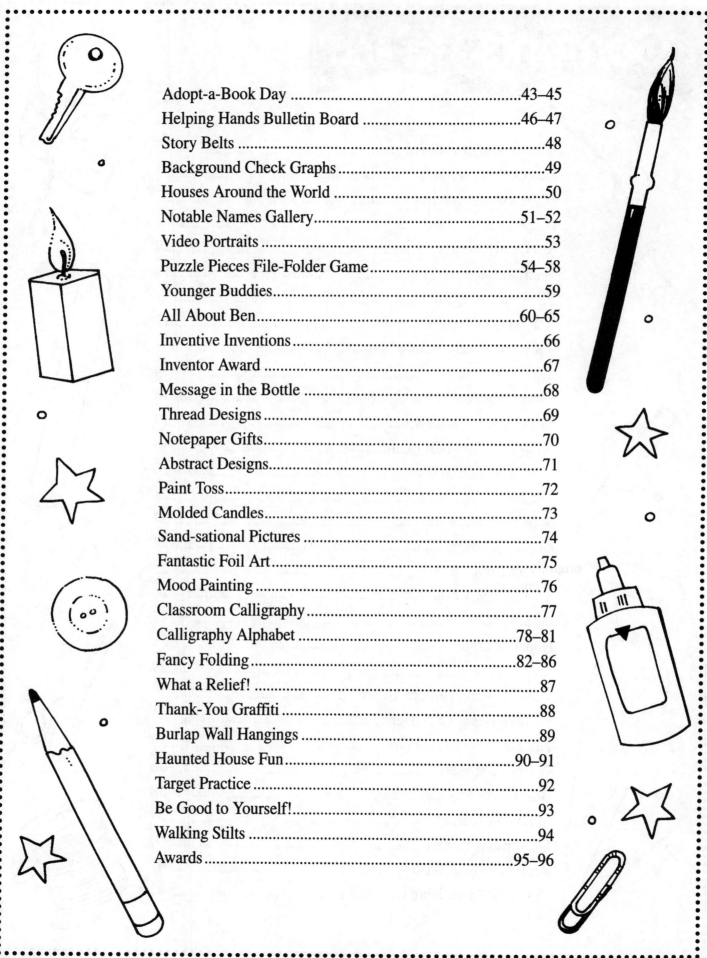

Sun Art Bulletin Board

MATERIALS:

12" x 18" bright-colored construction paper
objects collected outdoors and indoors
small stones or straight pins
yellow bulletin board paper
stapler

DIRECTIONS:

1. On a very sunny day, brainstorm with the class about the topic of the sun. Encourage students to identify the different roles the sun plays in our lives. Write the comments on a chalkboard. Discuss the class's ideas and decide together which ones are accurate and which ones need to be revised.

2. Introduce the following activity to the class. Inform them that they will do the first half of the work and the energy of the sun will do the other half. Begin by having students collect objects small enough to fit on 12" x 18" construction paper. Allow them plenty of time to walk around indoors as well as outdoors collecting their objects.

3. Ask students to choose a sheet of construction paper, go outdoors with it and their collections, and lay the paper flat on the ground. Have them arrange their collections on their papers and weight the objects in place using small stones. The stones should not be bigger than the objects. If the stones are too big, a straight pin stuck through the object and into the paper should work.

4. Leave the paper outdoors for at least one hour in direct sunlight. After the recommended time, students may take the objects off their papers and look at the results. The paper should have faded enough so that the outlines of the objects are clearly visible.

5. Experiment with different objects, different amounts of time in the sun, different times of day, and different colors of paper.

6. Staple bright yellow paper onto a bulletin board. Arrange the students' examples of sun art on the board under the title "Sun Creations." Write the question, "Can you guess what these objects are?" on the board as well. If desired, staple small cards to the bottom of the bulletin board with the answers written on them.

5

Land's End Lighthouse

MATERIALS:

empty oatmeal containers (cylindrical)
embroidery needles
sketch paper and pencils
paints and paintbrushes
collage materials
glue
"D" batteries
flashlight light bulbs
copper wire
masking tape

DIRECTIONS:

1. Collect and share with the students pictures of lighthouses throughout the world. Ask them to describe the reasons lighthouses are used. Ask students to explain why they are placed so close to the water.

2. Distribute one cylindrical oatmeal box and one embroidery needle to each student. Ask each child to use pencils and paper to create a design for a window for his or her lighthouse. When their designs are complete, they may sketch them onto their containers. The containers should be held upside down, so the open end becomes the bottom. Designs may then be sketched onto the top halves of the containers. This will be the window area, from which the light will shine. Remind students to make their windows large enough so that light will be able to shine through them.

3. Using a needle, demonstrate how to poke holes right next to one another along the pencil tracings of a window design. This will weaken the cardboard along the outline. Students can then gently push the cardboard along the perforations until it comes away from the container.

4. When all the windows have been poked out, students may choose colors for their lighthouses and paint them. When dry, the lighthouses may be decorated using collage materials and glue.

5. To make the light for the lighthouses, students will need to create a circuit using a "D" battery, a light bulb, two 6" lengths of wire, and some masking tape. Allow them time to experiment with their materials until they discover that taping one end of one wire to the negative end of the battery, taping one end of the other wire to the positive end of the battery, and joining both free ends to the base of the light bulb will light the bulb. To keep the bulb lit, they can tape the ends to the base of the bulb.

6. To light their lighthouses, students may simply place their lighthouses over their circuits. Turn off the lights and invite students to walk around the room and gaze at all the lighthouses shining in the dark.

Creative Projects

We're Going on a Dig

MATERIALS:

plaster of Paris
water
mixing bowls and spoons
disposable, wax-coated shallow bowls
small objects from around the room
oil
large containers filled with dirt (one for
    every three students)
spoons, brushes, and tweezers
scraps of paper, pencils, and tape
glue

DIRECTIONS:

1. Ask the class to tell what they know about archaeology. Explain to students that archaeology is the study of the life and culture of ancient peoples. Archaeologists study these peoples' lives by observing objects that they once used. They also study the types of houses in which they lived, the clothing they wore, and the food they ate. They try to discover the languages and customs of these peoples. Ask students to explain how archaeologists gather all this information.
2. Share a book with the class showing archaeologists on a dig, searching for and digging up artifacts. Then inform the class that they will be creating artifacts for their classmates to find and identify. Ask the class to walk around the room and find small objects they can use to make their own artifacts. Some suggested items are: key, brush, comb, crayon, scissor, feather, or fork.
3. Distribute plaster of Paris, water, bowls, and spoons to the class and have students follow the directions on the package for mixing the plaster of Paris. Have students pour the mixture into the shallow bowls. When the plaster begins to thicken, students should rub some oil onto their objects and then gently press them into the plaster and remove them. Objects should be washed immediately before the plaster dries on them.
4. When the plaster has dried, students may break up their artifacts into two or three pieces and choose a container of dirt in which to bury them. (There should be three students to each container, and all the pieces of an artifact should be buried in the same container.) Then distribute the tools and ask students to dig in a container of dirt in which they did not bury anything. Describe the care archaeologists use when digging and remind them to be as careful as possible.
5. As students find objects in the dirt, have them label their finds and place them together on a shelf or nearby table. When all the artifacts have been found, each group should piece together their finds. They may then glue the pieces together and identify the artifacts. Invite the groups to walk around the room looking at all the artifacts. Ask them to give some insights into the culture of the people who used each artifact. Discuss the comments.

Creative Projects

Outer Space Pictures

MATERIALS:

construction paper
crayons
blunt-edged plastic needles
tape

DIRECTIONS:

1. Explain to the class that they will be making outer space pictures. Ask them to close their eyes for a few minutes and imagine that they have been asked to participate in a flight to outer space. Their task is to observe all they can and describe in detail the sights they see.

2. When students have an image of what they will report, they may open their eyes and begin work on their pictures. Distribute a piece of paper to each student and place an assortment of crayons at each table.

3. Ask students to color their papers completely, using as many colors as they choose. When the papers are covered, students should color over their entire papers again, with black crayons. Both applications must be applied thickly.

4. Hand out blunt-edged plastic needles as students finish their coloring. Demonstrate how to use the needles as if they were pencils, lightly drawing them through the top crayon coatings. The base colors will show through as the black crayon layers are scratched.

5. Ask students to write detailed descriptions of their pictures and tape them to the bottom of their drawings. Display the outer space art on the wall for all to enjoy.

Creative Projects

Tie-Dyed T-Shirts

MATERIALS:

onions, beets, blueberries, spinach,
   and other vegetables and fruits
plastic knives
large pot
measuring cup
bowls
wooden spoons
white T-shirts
rubber bands

DIRECTIONS:

1. Ask volunteers to explain how colored dyes are made. Show students various vegetables and fruits, such as onions, beets, blueberries, and spinach, and inform them that colors can be made from things found in nature. Ask students to predict which colors will come from each of the vegetables and the fruit.

2. Have each child bring in one white T-shirt. Begin making the dyes by asking volunteers to peel the onions, cut the beets into small pieces, mash the blueberries, and tear the spinach into smaller bits. Place one cup of each item in a separate bowl.

3. Boil eight or more cups of water. Pour two cups of water over each vegetable or fruit. Stir gently and let sit for about 15 minutes.

4. While the dyes are steeping, students may twist their T-shirts and tie the twists in place with rubber bands, as shown.

5. When students are done, they may dip their T-shirts into the bowls. Different sections may be dipped into different bowls to create multicolored shirts.

6. Place the shirts in a clean area to dry. Students should not remove the rubber bands until the shirts are dry. Invite the class to observe the T-shirt colors and patterns.

9

Seed Mosaic

MATERIALS:

    seeds of many different varieties
    cardboard pieces
    glue

DIRECTIONS:

1. Divide the class into groups of four students each. Give each group a variety of seeds. Invite the students to look through them and create seed categories. Ask each group to share their categories with the class.

2. Discuss the various seeds with the class. Ask them to guess what type of plant might grow from each kind of seed. Then show students the packages each type came in. Ask them to describe how the seeds might be dispersed.

3. Give each student a piece of cardboard and some glue. Put more seeds on each table. Inform students that they will be making a mosaic of seeds on their cardboard pieces. They may first sketch out their pictures on the cardboard if they wish.

4. When the mosaics are complete, hang them on a wall. Ask students to share their work with the class.

Creative Projects

Environment Quilt

MATERIALS:

> fabric paint or markers
> twin-sized flat sheet
> tape

DIRECTIONS:

1. Ask students to consider the following thought: "If I could do anything to help the environment, I would . . ." Give each child a piece of paper and a pencil and ask them to sketch out their ideas.

2. Encourage the class to share their sketches with each other. Students may ask questions and make comments.

3. Next, lay out a twin-sized flat sheet and tape the edges to the floor. Divide the sheet into an equal number of squares. Ask two or three students at a time to come to the sheet and, using the fabric paints or markers, draw their ideas for making Earth a better place to live. Students should provide mottoes or slogans to match their drawings.

4. When all the students have drawn their illustrations and written their slogans, hang the quilt for the class's inspection. Discuss their ideas.

5. When it is time to take the quilt down, hold a lottery and allow the winning student to take it home, or donate the quilt to the library or science room.

Crayon-Shaving Pictures

MATERIALS:

9" x 12" pieces of waxed paper
scissors
old crayons
iron
glue

colored construction paper
vegetable peelers or graters
old newspapers
9" x 12" colored construction paper
tape

DIRECTIONS:

1. Ask the class to brainstorm about the topic of the seasons. Encourage them to call out comments, and ask a volunteer to write the ideas on the chalkboard. When all the comments have been made, categorize them according to whether they pertain to winter, spring, summer, or fall.

2. Inform the class that they will be making pictures that reflect their favorite seasons. Distribute construction paper and scissors to each student. Ask them to choose a season and cut out outlines of objects relevant to their chosen season. For example, if a student chooses winter as his or her favorite season, that student might cut out a snowperson, an evergreen, and a bundled-up person.

3. After the objects are cut out, distribute one sheet of waxed paper to each student. Tell students to arrange their objects on this layer of paper.

4. Give out vegetable peelers or graters and old crayons with their wrappers removed. Demonstrate to the class how to rub the peeler along the length of a crayon to create shavings.

5. Tell students to use these shavings to decorate their pictures. For example, for a fall picture, a student may choose to decorate a tree trunk with red, orange, yellow, and brown shavings and use green shavings for grass.

6. When the shavings have been made and put in place, have each student place a second sheet of waxed paper over the picture. Over this, lay approximately four sheets of old newspaper.

7. Slide a hot iron over the newspapers for about ten seconds. Lift the newspapers to be sure the shavings are all melted. If not, use the iron for a few more seconds over the spots that need more heat.

8. Have students frame their pictures with construction paper. Demonstrate how to fold a paper in half and cut out a rectangle in the middle, leaving a 1" frame. Glue one frame to the back and one to the front. Tape the pictures to a window so that the sun reflects the colors into the classroom.

Creative Projects

Recycled Goods Picture Frame

MATERIALS:

- small and clean bits of junk
- craft sticks
- glue
- cardboard pieces
- waxed paper
- paints and paintbrushes
- photographs
- yarn

DIRECTIONS:

1. Discuss with the class the importance of recycling. Ask if there are recycling programs in their neighborhoods. Discuss the benefits of recycling certain items, such as glass, paper, and plastic.

2. Inform the class that they will be making picture frames and decorating the frames with recycled materials they've collected. Since the frames will be about 2" wide, the materials should be small. These materials should be clean and have no sharp edges.

3. To make the frame, distribute cardboard, waxed paper, craft sticks, and glue to the class. Each student should have four sets of four craft sticks. Work should be done on a base of cardboard covered with a piece of waxed paper. Demonstrate how to glue four sticks side by side. When they dry, students can arrange them so the top and bottom overlap the right and left sides by 1". Then students can glue them in place.

4. When the joints have dried, the frames are ready to paint. When the frames are dry, students may decorate them with their collected materials.

5. Ask students to bring in a favorite photograph or magazine picture to glue to the frame. Instruct students to turn their frames over and squeeze a line of glue along the left and right sides. The photograph or picture may then be pressed into place and any excess cut off.

6. A small loop may be added to the top of the frame for hanging. Have each student cut a 4" length of yarn and glue the ends to the back of the frame at the top.

Class Pets

Animals are a wonderful way to introduce students to nature. Have a class discussion about various animals that might be suitable for a class pet. Some suggested animals are: lizards, frogs, turtles, rabbits, gerbils, and ants.

After a pet (or pets) have been agreed on, talk about what preparations need to be made before acquiring the animal. For example, if the class pet is to be a rabbit, it will need a hutch, food, a water bowl, and a litter box. If possible, have students work together to build a home for the animal.

Have the class work up a schedule beforehand for taking care of the animal. Be sure to include vacations, during which time the animal will need to go home with one or more of the students.

Ask the students to research the habits and nature of the chosen animal. Have students write up short reports that tell about the animal and explain why they think it would make a good class pet.

If possible, go on a field trip to the pet store (or to wherever the animal is to be obtained). Take a class vote if there is more than one of the selected animals from which to choose.

After the animal has been living in the classroom for several weeks, have a follow-up discussion on the long-term responsibilities of having a pet. Ask volunteers to tell what they have liked or disliked about the class pet, and what things about caring for the pet they did or did not expect.

Creative Projects

Global Awareness Bulletin Board

MATERIALS:
- crayons or markers
- glue
- oaktag
- scissors
- lined paper
- stapler

DIRECTIONS:

1. Reproduce the globe on page 16 once for each student. Have students color the globes, mount them on oaktag, and cut them out.

2. Ask each student to research a current environmental topic. The issue may be local, national, or worldwide. Give students time to research in the school library, and encourage them to visit their town library as well.

3. When a student has gathered as much information as possible about his or her topic, have him or her write a short report about the issue. Review each draft individually to discuss content, grammar, and spelling.

4. Have each student trace the oaktag globe onto lined paper as many times as necessary to accommodate the length of his or her report. Then ask each child to carefully copy the final draft of his or her report onto the lined paper globes.

5. Staple the pages together in order, placing the oaktag globe on top as a cover. Have each student write the title of the report and his or her name on the cover.

6. Attach the globes to a bulletin board under the heading "Global Awareness."

Creative Projects

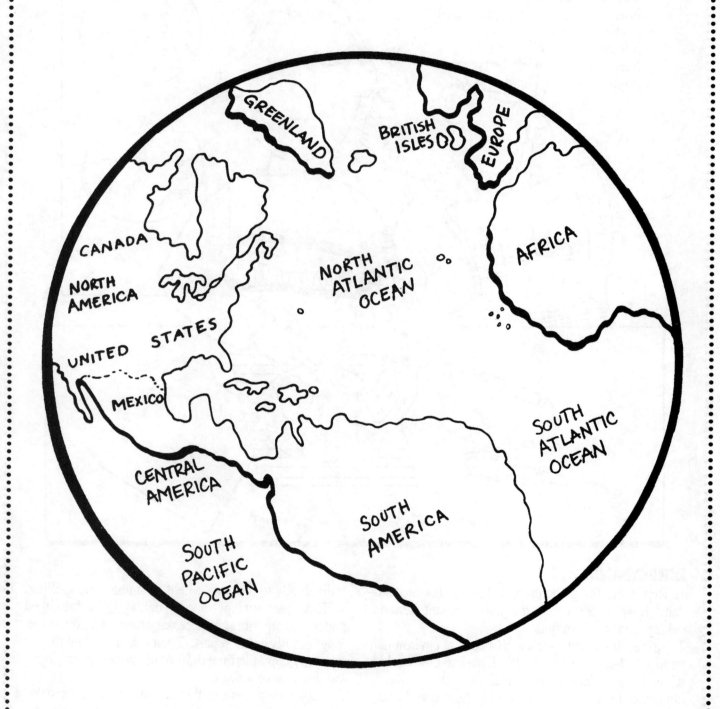

GREENLAND

BRITISH
ISLES

EUROPE

CANADA

AFRICA

NORTH
AMERICA

NORTH
ATLANTIC
OCEAN

UNITED STATES

MEXICO

SOUTH
ATLANTIC
OCEAN

CENTRAL
AMERICA

SOUTH
AMERICA

SOUTH
PACIFIC
OCEAN

Visitors from Outer Space

MATERIALS:
mural paper
crayons or markers
paints and
    paintbrushes
tape

DIRECTIONS:
1. Give each student a sheet of mural paper slightly longer than the length of his or her body. Working in pairs, students should lay down on the mural paper and have their partners trace the outlines of their bodies.
2. Tell students that they are going to imagine that they are visitors from outer space. Students may either make up a home planet or choose one from our solar system. Have students color or paint their mural tracings to look like people from outer space.
3. When the murals have been completed, ask each student to write a short biography of his or her space person. Tell students to include details of daily life, likes and dislikes, and why the visitor has chosen to come to planet Earth.
4. Encourage students to show their murals and read their biographies to the rest of the class. Then attach the murals and biographies to classroom walls or mount them in a school hallway for everyone to see.

Creative Projects

Silhouettes Bulletin Board

MATERIALS:

black construction paper   tape
filmstrip projector   pencil
white construction paper   scissors
white marker or pencil   glue
purple bulletin board paper

DIRECTIONS:

1. Place a chair sideways next to a wall. Ask a student to sit straight up in the chair. Then tape a piece of black construction paper to the wall behind his or her head.

2. Shine the lamp from a filmstrip projector onto the student's head. Adjust the beam of light until the student's profile fits in the center of the black paper.

Using a pencil, trace around the student's profile.

3. When the tracing is done, have the student cut out his or her profile. Repeat for the rest of the class.

4. When all the profiles are cut out, students may mount them on white construction paper.

5. Ask students to think of the quality they like best in themselves. It may be a physical characteristic, a personality characteristic, or anything they choose. Encourage students to share their chosen features with the class. Each student may then write his or her best quality in white marker or pencil onto the silhouette.

6. Staple purple bulletin board paper to the bulletin board. Arrange the silhouettes on the board. If desired, title the bulletin board "Our Best Qualities."

    Creative Projects

Into the Future Scenes

MATERIALS:
crayons or markers
scissors
construction paper
glue

DIRECTIONS:
1. Reproduce the window art on page 20 once for each student. Ask students to color their windows. Demonstrate how to cut out the window panes so that only the sash is left.
2. On a separate piece of construction paper, have each student create a scene that shows what he or she would like to be doing in the future. Students may choose to show a job, a hobby, a family scene, a location, or anything else that gives a glimpse of how they imagine their futures might be.
3. Students may then squeeze a line of glue around the edges of their pictures and lay the window cutout over them, lining up all the edges. Display the windows around the room and invite students to look at them and guess what type of future their classmates envision for themselves.

Creative Projects

The Masks We Wear

MATERIALS:

brown paper grocery bags
crayons or markers
collage materials
glue
scrap paper
scissors

DIRECTIONS:

1. Ask the class to identify the emotions they experienced during the past week. As each student names a new emotion, ask him or her to write it out on the chalkboard. Identify other emotions if students overlook them. Encourage the more dramatically inclined students to use body language to convey each of the emotions listed on the chalkboard.

2. Discuss with the class how emotions can change depending on a situation or an event. Ask students to name events that might trigger the emotions they named. Talk about ways to diffuse certain situations that involve extreme emotions such as anger and sadness. Ask students to describe ways in which they help themselves feel better.

3. Inform the class that they will be making emotion masks. Distribute grocery bags to each student and provide crayons, markers, collage materials, glue, paper, and scissors to the class. Allow students to choose the types of masks they wish to make.

4. Have students open the grocery bags and set them on tables with the open ends down and the bottoms facing up.

5. After students have finished decorating and personalizing their masks, ask students to stand their masks up around the room and then go browsing through them. See if students can identify which emotion is being illustrated by each mask.

21

MATERIALS:

18" x 24" flannel pieces
flannel scraps
scissors
fabric glue
yarn

DIRECTIONS:

1. Divide the class into groups of three. Ask the groups to brainstorm about ways of staying healthy. After five minutes, ask the groups to share their thoughts with the class. Be sure topics such as nutrition, sleep, exercise, making informed decisions, self-esteem, and handling stress and other emotions are mentioned.

2. Inform the groups that they will be making banners to illustrate a health issue. Ask them to choose one to illustrate on a banner. Distribute one flannel rectangle to each group, along with the flannel scraps, scissors, and glue. Groups should then use the flannel scraps to create banners showing some aspects of the issues they chose.

3. When the banners are finished, demonstrate how to fold 1" over to the back and glue the fold down along the edge. Insert a 40" length of yarn through the folded edge and knot the ends together, as shown. This will enable the groups to hang their banners.

4. When the banners are hung, ask one person from each group to describe their work and explain what it represents.

Healthy Choices

Have a class discussion about healthful eating habits. Begin by asking each student to write down what he or she ate and drank in the last 24 hours, organized by meals and snacks.

Ask volunteers to share their lists with the rest of the class. Analyze the lists to see if each participant has had his or her share of the required daily allowance of vitamins and minerals. Check the approximate fat content for each list to see whether it is no more than 30% of a student's total daily calories.

Go over the food pyramid with the class. Discuss the number of daily servings necessary for each food group. Ask volunteers to name sample foods for each food group, and categorize the comments on a chalkboard.

Ask each student to try to fulfill the requirements of the food pyramid each day for a week. Tell students to log the foods they have eaten during that week. At the end of the time period, review the lists individually with each student to determine if he or she was successful. (Students may also enjoy including their teacher in this class effort!)

Reproduce the figures on page 24 as many times as necessary to have one fruit or vegetable for each student. When a student has successfully completed a week of healthful eating, have him or her color in a fruit or vegetable and write his or her name on the front.

Attach the fruits and vegetables to a section of a bulletin board under the title "We're Making Healthful Choices!"

Healthy Choices

Peanut Butter Balls

MATERIALS:

2 cups peanut butter
4 cups powdered milk
2 cups honey
wooden spoon

teaspoons
large mixing bowl
waxed paper
napkins

DIRECTIONS:

1. Ask two students to mix together in a large mixing bowl 2 cups of peanut butter with 2 cups of honey until well blended.
2. Have two more students slowly stir in 4 cups of powdered milk.
3. Ask five volunteers to take teaspoons of the mixture and roll them into small balls. Place the balls on waxed paper.
4. Allow time for the balls to harden. Serve and enjoy!

Stained-Glass Fractions

MATERIALS:

- black construction paper
- pencils
- rulers
- scissors
- different colors of cellophane
- glue
- transparent tape

DIRECTIONS:

1. Distribute a piece of black construction paper and a pencil to each student. Explain to the students that they will be making stained-glass designs, but they must make them according to the following dimensions: 1/4 must be covered by one color, 1/8 must be covered by another color, 1/2 must be covered by a third color, and the last 1/8 must be covered by the same color as was used for the 1/4 section. (You may change the instructions to any fraction combination.)

2. Encourage students to use rulers so that they measure out their designs accurately. When each student has sketched a design on his or her paper, ask the child to share it with a classmate. Have the students check each other's work.

3. When the dimensions are correct, students may cut out the areas to be filled with colored cellophane. Then students may cut pieces of colored cellophane large enough to fit into each open space in their designs.

4. Demonstrate how to squeeze a line of glue around each section and lay a piece of colored cellophane over it. If the cellophane goes over the outside edges, students may cut off the excess when the glue has dried.

5. Tape the stained glass designs to a window where the sun can shine through the colored cellophane.

Distance Drivers

MATERIALS:

old handkerchiefs or squares of fabric,
    approximately 12" x 12"
hole puncher
10" long strips of yarn or thin
    string
weights, such as nuts or bolts
chalk
ruler or measuring tape

DIRECTIONS:

1. Distribute an old handkerchief or fabric scrap to each student to use to make a miniparachute. Demonstrate how to punch a hole in each corner of the fabric, about 1" in from the edge of the fabric.

2. Show students how to thread a 10" length of yarn or string into each hole and knot it securely. Make sure the knots are tight.

3. Ask students to think of objects that can be used to weigh down their parachutes, such as small nuts or bolts. Have each student twist the four free ends of the yarn lengths together and tie them to the weights.

4. Take the class outside and inform them that they will be measuring the distances their parachutes float. Students should mark the spot where they stand with chalk before they throw their parachutes into the air. When the parachutes come down, students will mark the spot on which they land.

5. Using a ruler, a measuring tape, or other unit of measurement (standard and nonstandard), students can then measure the distance between where they tossed their parachutes and where they landed.

6. Ask students to create a chart that will show the different distances measured. Which distances were represented the most? The least? The same? What might happen on a windier day? A still day?

27

Human Computers

MATERIALS:
large appliance box
paper towel rolls and old newspapers
masking tape
paint and brushes
scissors
pencil and paper

DIRECTIONS:

1. Help the class create their own human computer. Begin by collecting a large appliance box, some paper towel rolls, and some old newspapers.

2. Cut the back of the box off, leaving the top, bottom, and three sides. Use paper towel rolls and newspapers to create arms, legs, hands, feet, and any facial features the class wishes to include. Tape the limbs and features onto the box.

3. Ask volunteers to paint the computer. A group meeting held before painting will allow time for students to decide which colors to use and whether to paint various features on the computer, such as clothing, buttons and knobs, and lights.

4. About chest high on a student of average height, cut a slit in the front of the box. This will be the spot where students may give the computer their questions and where the computer will send its answers back. Demonstrate to the class how a student can stand in the box and act as the human computer.

5. Choose one student to go inside the box. Choose another student to approach the computer and give it a question, either on a piece of paper or verbally. If questions are given verbally, the student inside the computer can write the problem down on a piece of paper kept inside the computer. When he or she has answered the problem, the student computer can send the answer back out to the questioner through the slit.

6. Math concepts that lend themselves to this activity include rounding off, addition, subtraction, multiplication, division, fractions, decimals, percents, perimeter, area, and averages.

Creative Projects

Fraction Pie

MATERIALS:

2 cups sifted flour
2/3 cup shortening
6 apples
2 tablespoons flour
dash of nutmeg and of salt
large mixing bowls
wooden spoon
rolling pin

1 teaspoon salt
cold water
3/4 cup sugar
1/2 teaspoon cinnamon
2 tablespoons butter
small mixing bowl
pie tin
plastic knives, forks

DIRECTIONS:

1. Make this apple pie to help students gain hands-on experience with fractions. This pie will divide into eight good-sized pieces. To make more, students will need to help you make a second pie, multiplying the ingredients amounts accordingly.

2. Sift 2 cups of flour and 1 teaspoon of salt together in a large bowl. Using plastic knives, cut in 2/3 cup of shortening until the mixture resembles coarse crumbs.

3. Sprinkle a tablespoon of cold water over a portion of the dough and work it in with a fork. Continue sprinkling water onto small portions of the dough and working it in with the fork. When the dough is completely moist, form it into a ball with your hands. Divide the dough in half, one for the top crust and one for the bottom.

4. Flour a flat surface and place the first dough ball on it. Sprinkle a rolling pin with flour and roll the dough about 1/8" thick. Then gently pick it up and lay it in the bottom of an 8" pie tin. Repeat with the other dough ball and lay it aside.

5. Cut six apples into small chunks and place them in a large bowl. Combine the 3/4 cup of sugar, 2 tablespoons of flour, 1/2 teaspoon of cinnamon, and a dash of nutmeg and of salt in a small bowl. Mix the combined ingredients with the apple chunks.

6. Fill the pie tin with the mixture. Cut 2 tablespoons of butter into smaller bits and place them around the top of the apple mixture. Lay the second rolled dough layer on top of the apple mixture. Tuck the top layer under the rim of the bottom crust and press the two together with the tines of a fork.

7. Bake in a 400°F oven for approximately 50 minutes. Let cool, then serve and enjoy!

Creative Projects

Venn Diagram Bulletin Board

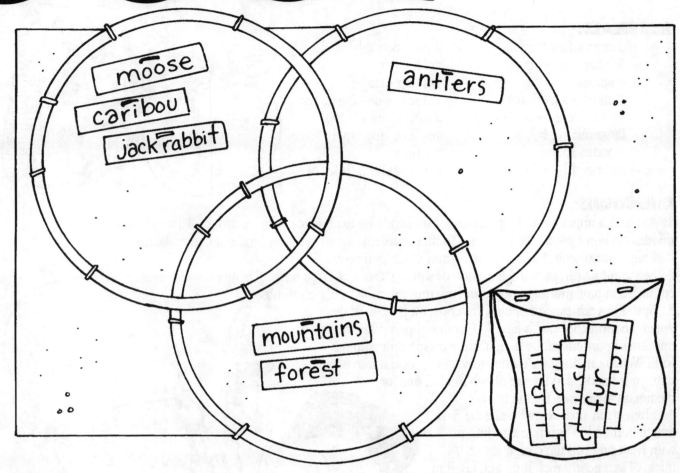

MATERIALS:

    light-colored bulletin board paper
    stapler
    three different colors of yarn
    1" x 4" strips of oaktag
    markers
    clear plastic bag

DIRECTIONS:

1. Staple paper to a bulletin board, low enough so students will be able to manipulate the objects upon it. Cut 5' lengths of three different colors of yarn and staple these to the board in Venn diagram form, making sure the circles overlap.
2. Create three categories for the Venn diagram, such as object names, concepts, physical characteristics, place names, or vocabulary. Write category words on 1" x 4" strips of oaktag and staple them into the proper category circles including the overlapping areas. Do not write the category titles on the circles. Staple a plastic bag onto the bulletin board, near the base and off to the side.
3. Demonstrate how to use the board. Ask a student to read the words in one of the circles. Ask the class what the words have in common. Then have them create a name for the category. Repeat the process for the other circles. When all the categories are named, ask the students if the category titles correctly identify the words in each circle, especially the overlapping areas. If so, ask a student to write them on oaktag strips and staple the strips to the top of each circle.
4. On consecutive days, staple new words in the circles and encourage the students to create their own titles. They can write their guesses down on paper and place them in the bag at the bottom of the board.
5. After reviewing the guesses with the class, ask them to vote on category titles that would encompass all the words in each circle. Or place category words in the bag on the board and encourage students to sort them themselves.

Creative Projects

Positive/Negative Designs

MATERIALS:

    white and black construction paper
    pencils
    scissors
    glue

DIRECTIONS:

1. Divide the class into groups of four students each. Distribute paper, pencils, and scissors to each group.
2. Demonstrate how to fold a sheet of white construction paper into fourths. When students have folded their papers, inform them that they will be creating pictures that have positive and negative sides to them.
3. Ask if anyone in the class has heard the terms *positive* and *negative* and can explain them for everyone. If not, explain that in photography, the negative print reverses the relation of light and dark shades of the subject. A positive print is one in which the light and dark shades correspond to those of the subject. If possible, show the class some examples of photographs and their negatives, so that students can see the inverse relationship between the positive prints and the negatives.

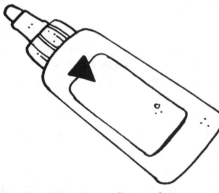

4. Show students how to draw a design on one side of their folded papers and then cut it out. The design should be done in the center of the folded paper, leaving the edges intact.
5. When the designs have been cut out, tell students to place the cutout pieces off to one side. Open up the folded papers and have students cut them along the fold marks. Ask students to choose a piece of black construction paper.
6. Have students glue their design frames to the black papers, placing the cutout design between each one, as follows: black papers should be placed on a flat surface with the longer edge closest to them. They should glue the first design frame into the upper left corner of the paper, then glue a cutout next to it, then another frame, then another cutout, as shown. Have students repeat the procedure for the bottom half of the paper, but ask them to begin with a cutout in the bottom left corner.
7. When the pictures are finished, encourage students to share their work and make any comments about the finished product, such as what it might resemble and the processes used. This activity is also a good way to illustrate symmetry (by cutting out symmetrical designs).

           Creative Projects

The Borrowers Minihouse

MATERIALS:

cartons
cardboard
scissors
masking tape
wallpaper samples
construction paper
crayons or markers

glue
paints and paintbrushes
collage materials
pint and quart milk and juice containers
transparent tape
fabric scraps
fabric glue

DIRECTIONS:

1. Read the book *The Borrowers* by Mary Norton (published by Harcourt Brace Jovanovich, 1953) with the class. Inform students that they will be creating a home that would be suitable for a tiny family such as the Borrowers.

2. Ask each student to bring in a carton from home that can be divided into appropriate rooms, such as a kitchen, a living room, bedrooms, and a bathroom.

3. Distribute cardboard pieces, scissors, and masking tape. To divide the rooms and make walls, students can cut pieces that are the same length and width as their boxes. Remind students to cut out windows for their homes as well. Distribute wallpaper samples and books from home improvement stores and interior decorating companies. Or students may create their own wallpaper using construction paper and crayons or markers.

4. Have students glue the wallpaper to the walls.

Encourage students to be creative in their decorating. They may wish to paint rooms or use collage materials to brighten the walls.

5. Distribute cardboard containers for students to make furniture for the house. For example, a half-pint milk container may be used as a bed. Another one may be turned into a couch.

6. Cover the furniture with fabric scraps that match the walls in the rooms for which they are intended. Fabric glue can be used to join fabric scraps together to make pillows and rugs and other large items, such as tablecloths and curtains. Scrap materials may be used to create details such as dishes, toys, pictures in frames, and books.

7. When the houses are finished, ask students to place them on their tables. Give them about 15 minutes to browse through them. Gather together to discuss construction techniques, decorating tips, and room arrangements.

Poetry in Motion

MATERIALS:

scissors
pencils
large sheets of oaktag
12" x 18" construction paper
crayons or markers

DIRECTIONS:

1. Reproduce the art on pages 34, 35, and 36 once each. Ask volunteers to cut out the art, being careful to stay on the lines. Then ask other volunteers to trace each pattern onto oaktag four times to make stencils. Cut out the stencils.

2. Distribute construction paper to the class, along with pencils and crayons or markers. Demonstrate how to hold a stencil on the paper to the left of the center. Trace around the stencil onto the paper, then lift the stencil and move it about 1" to the right. Trace again. Repeat the procedure at least three times.

3. Show students the finished product. Ask them to describe what they see. It should appear as though the object drawn with the stencil is moving.

4. When students have traced their chosen stencils several times, encourage them to color in their drawings. Students may wish to color in a background.

5. Ask the class to observe their drawings quietly at this time. If any words or images come to them as they look, they may write them down on paper. After a few minutes have passed, ask students to create a short poem. If possible, they should use the words and images they recorded.

6. Poems may be written on the same paper as the "motion pictures." When everyone has finished, encourage students to share their poems with the class. Display the work on a bulletin board under the title "Poetry in Motion."

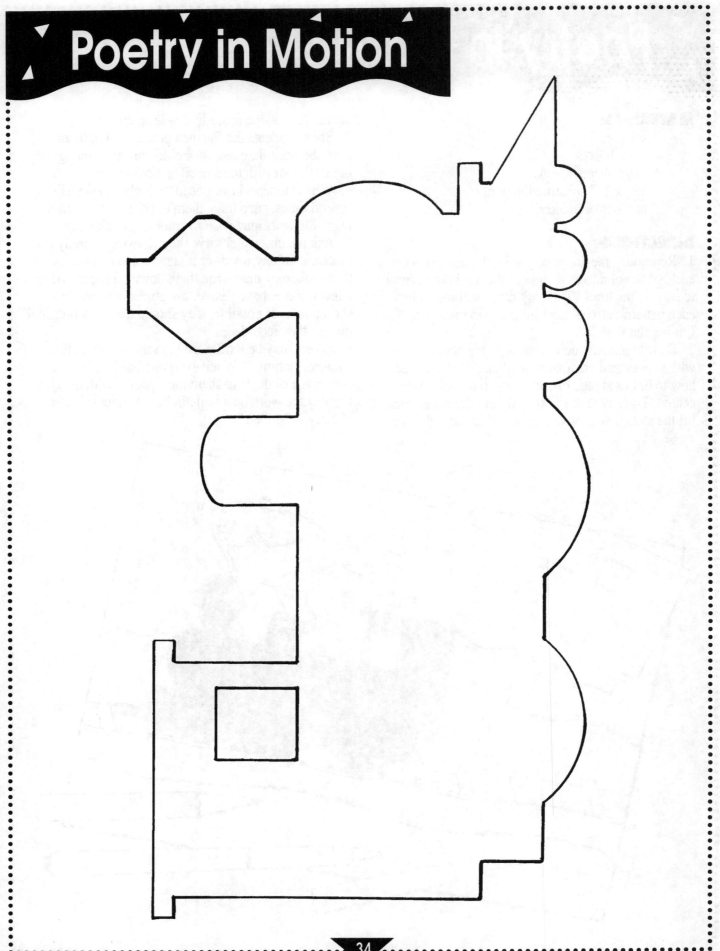

Creative Projects

Poetry in Motion

Best Books Mobiles

MATERIALS:

scissors
pencils
crayons and markers
large sheets of oaktag
yarn
fabric scraps
collage materials
clean junk (containers, wrapping
   paper, lids, etc.)
glue
hole puncher

DIRECTIONS:

1. Reproduce the art on page 38 four times for each student. Ask students to name some books they have enjoyed reading in the past year. On the chalkboard write their names next to their nominations.

2. Ask the class to take five minutes to think about the book they named and consider the following three categories: favorite character, setting, and plot.

3. Distribute four book patterns to each student. Inform the students that they will be making mobiles about the books they have named as their favorites. On the first book pattern, each student will draw a picture of his or her favorite character and explain why this character is special. On the second book pattern, each student will write about the setting of the book and draw a picture illustrating it. On the third book pattern, each student will write about the plot of the book (without giving away the ending).

4. On the last book pattern, each student may illustrate or write about anything from his or her favorite book. Possibilities include a recommendation, a sample of art from the book, a diary entry stating a point of view different from that of the main character, or a mock interview with a character from the book. Have students punch a hole at the top of each book pattern.

5. Allow students to decide on a shape or device from which to hang their book patterns. Students should create something that represents their favorite book. For example, a student who enjoyed the book *James and the Giant Peach* by Roald Dahl (published by Knopf, 1961) may want to make a giant peach from which to hang the book patterns. Four holes could be punched at the bottom of the peach. Then the book patterns should be tied to the peach using yarn.

6. Ask each student to share their mobiles with the class. The mobiles may then be hung in the classroom or donated to the school library for a semester.

Creative Projects

Best Books Mobiles

Mountain Journals

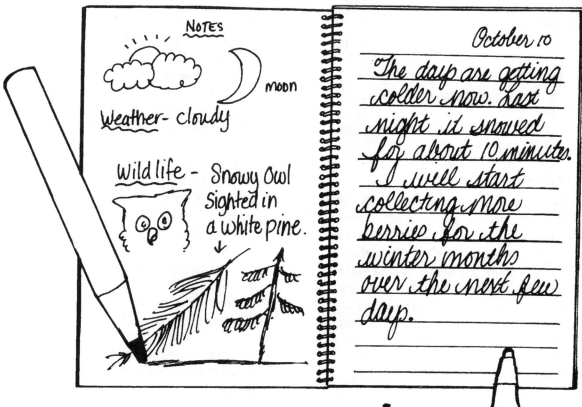

NOTES

Weather- cloudy

moon

Wild life - Snowy Owl sighted in a white pine.

October 10

The days are getting colder now. Last night it snowed for about 10 minutes. I will start collecting more berries for the winter months over the next few days.

Have the class read the book *My Side of the Mountain* by Jean Craighead George (published by Dutton, 1959). Ask volunteers to talk about what life was like for Sam as he tried to live on his own in the wilderness.

Tell students that they are going to keep journals about imaginary experiences in the wilderness. Ask each child to bring in a composition book or some other type of notebook that would make a good journal. Have each student think of a place where he or she would like to go, without depending on anyone else.

Give students time in the library to research their chosen locations. For example, if a student chooses to live in the Canadian Rockies, that student should research the climate there, what foods may be found there naturally, whether there are caves or other types of shelters, and whether or not it is possible to survive a winter there.

Provide students with an opportunity to write in their journals for about 15 minutes each day. If desired, ask students to take their journals home on nights when no homework has been assigned, or on weekends.

After a predesignated amount of time (such as one month) has passed, collect the journals. Try to review the journal with each student for content, grammar, and spelling. Ask volunteers to share several entries with the rest of the class. Then place the journals in the class reading center for all to enjoy.

Illuminated Stories

MATERIALS:

thick white paper (suitable for painting)
calligraphy pens
black ink
paints and paintbrushes
markers
two thin pieces of metal (approximately 9" x 12")

DIRECTIONS:

1. Have a class discussion about the history of written stories. Explain that the first manuscripts were probably written around 2700 B.C. These stories were written on papyrus, which was made from a plant growing around the Nile River in Egypt. Later cultures used wax tablets and parchment paper for writing stories.

2. Tell students that during the Middle Ages, monks wrote and illuminated manuscripts. These manuscripts were written in calligraphy, with fancy initial capital letters. Illustrations decorated these manuscripts, and often gold or silver leafing was used as well. Monks would divide the work into separate areas: one group made the parchment; another group wrote the stories; another group designed and illustrated the stories; and a final group bound the pages together to make the books.

3. Take the class to the library to see some examples of illuminated manuscripts. Point out the different styles of decoration that are used.

4. Ask students to write out a short story on composition paper. Review all the stories before students begin making them into illuminated manuscripts.

5. Distribute paper, calligraphy pens, and black ink to the class. Have children use calligraphy writing to write out their stories onto sturdy white paper.

6. When the ink has dried, provide students with paints and paintbrushes to use to decorate their manuscripts.

7. Collect the completed stories and place them together to make a class book. To make front and back covers for the book, you may wish to use two thin pieces of metal cut to size. The metal may be punched out and then painted to imitate an authentic illuminated manuscript cover.

When the sun rose over the garden that morning, I saw the watering can hiding behind a

Really Creative Writing

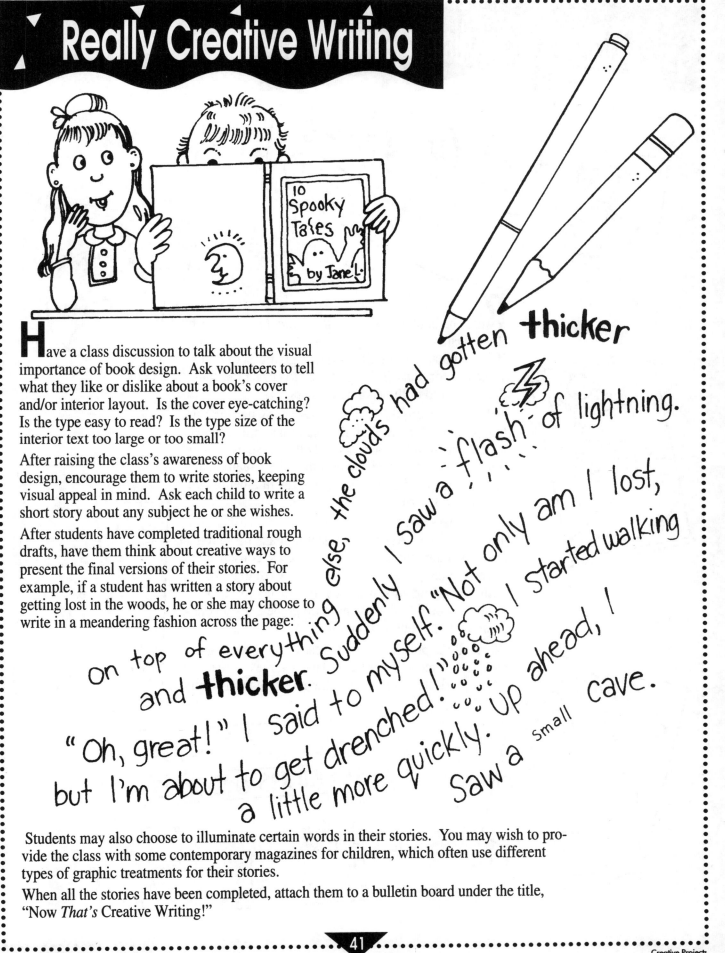

Have a class discussion to talk about the visual importance of book design. Ask volunteers to tell what they like or dislike about a book's cover and/or interior layout. Is the cover eye-catching? Is the type easy to read? Is the type size of the interior text too large or too small?

After raising the class's awareness of book design, encourage them to write stories, keeping visual appeal in mind. Ask each child to write a short story about any subject he or she wishes.

After students have completed traditional rough drafts, have them think about creative ways to present the final versions of their stories. For example, if a student has written a story about getting lost in the woods, he or she may choose to write in a meandering fashion across the page:

else, the clouds had gotten **thicker**

Suddenly I saw a flash of lightning.

"Not only am I lost,

I started walking

on top of everything

and **thicker**.

"Oh, great!" I said to myself.

but I'm about to get drenched!"

a little more quickly.

Up ahead, I

saw a small cave.

Students may also choose to illuminate certain words in their stories. You may wish to provide the class with some contemporary magazines for children, which often use different types of graphic treatments for their stories.

When all the stories have been completed, attach them to a bulletin board under the title, "Now *That's* Creative Writing!"

41

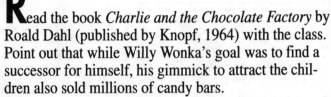

Read the book *Charlie and the Chocolate Factory* by Roald Dahl (published by Knopf, 1964) with the class. Point out that while Willy Wonka's goal was to find a successor for himself, his gimmick to attract the children also sold millions of candy bars.

Ask volunteers to think of the ways candy bars or other things are sold today. Tell the class that while contests held by fast-food restaurants and other businesses may offer a wonderful prize, these companies usually wind up making a large profit because of the number of people who participate.

Tell the class that they are going to be advertising executives for a day. Ask each student to make up a product to sell and then think of ways to generate consumer interest in the product. Students may wish to make posters showing what print advertisements for their products would look like, make up jingles, or videotape commercials about their products.

When all the presentations are ready, invite another class in to watch. Afterwards, take a survey to see which products were received the most enthusiastically.

Help salvage books from the class or school library by holding an "Adopt-a-Book Day." Explain to students that books often need repair work, because of mistreatment or frequent use. Remove several books from the class library that are in need of repair. Show students how to use strong tape to fix books whose interiors have separated from their covers.

Students may wish to make new covers for books whose covers have been removed. Using a piece of construction paper cut to fit around the front and back of the book with flaps to hold the cover in place, have a student draw a picture from the book and hand letter the title and credits. When the work is completed, laminate both sides of the cover. Then fold it around the book and tape in place.

Have students look through the class library for other books that need to be repaired. If possible, set up a meeting with the school librarian to see if students may repair those books as well.

Reproduce the book plates on page 44 as many times as necessary. Allow students to color and fill in a book plate and glue it inside the back cover (or another appropriate spot) on each book they repair.

When the project is completed, reproduce and fill in the certificate on page 45 once for each student.

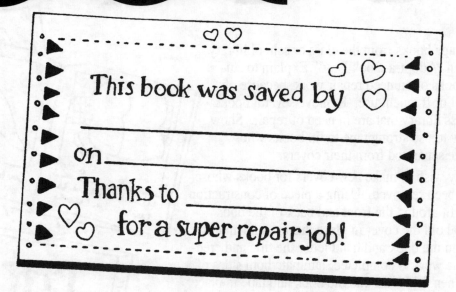

This book was saved by

_____

on_____

Thanks to _____

for a super repair job!

This book was saved by

_____

on_____

Thanks to _____

for a super repair job!

This book was saved by

_____

on_____

Thanks to _____

for a super repair job!

Adopt-a-Book Day!

Presented to

_____

_____

Date

_____

Teacher's name

Thanks for all your help!

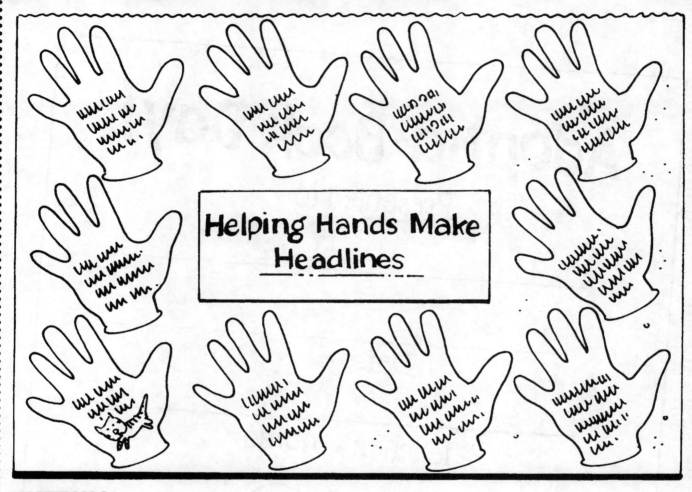

MATERIALS:

scissors
old newspapers
stapler

DIRECTIONS:

1. Reproduce the hand art on page 47 once for each student. Have student cut out the hands.
2. Discuss with the class what a "good deed" is. Talk about the term "good Samaritan." Ask students to name some good deeds they have done recently. How does doing something good for someone else make them feel? Would they feel the same way if they were made to do the same thing?
3. On the paper hands, ask each student to write about a good deed he or she has done. Encourage students to select the deeds of which they are the most proud. If there is room on their hands, students may draw small pictures to illustrate their good deeds.
4. Cover a bulletin board with old newspapers. Staple the students' paper hands around the board. Title the bulletin board, "Helping Hands Make Headlines."
5. When a student performs another good deed that he or she would like to share with the class, the student may write up another helping hand and staple it over his or her previous hand on the board. (Be sure to staple just along the top so past deeds can still be read.)

Helping Hands Bulletin Board

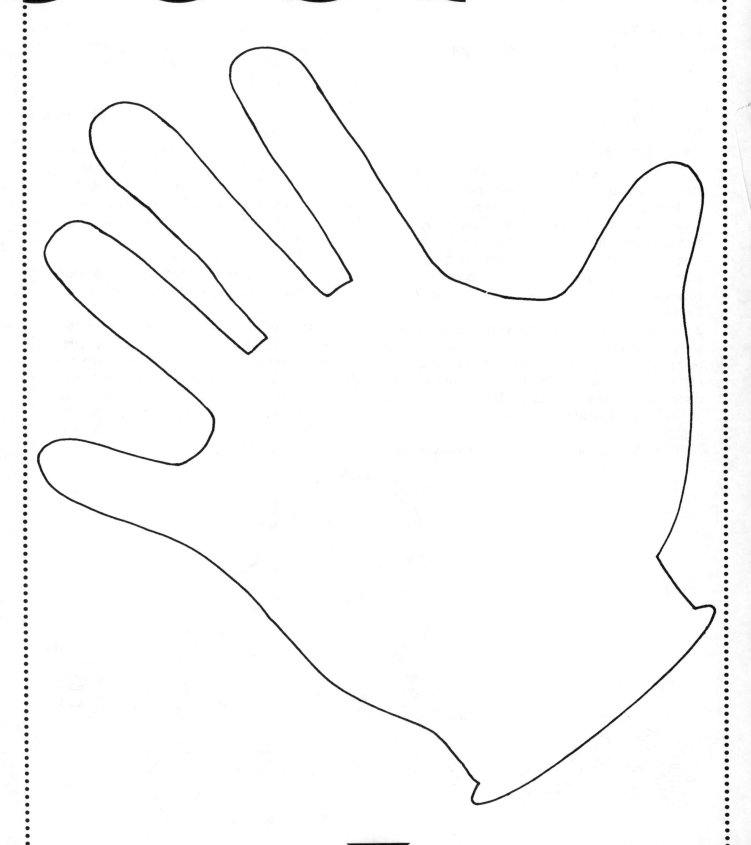

Creative Projects

Story Belts

MATERIALS:

12" x 18" colored construction paper
scissors
glue
pencils
colored yarn

DIRECTIONS:

1. Ask the class to explain ways in which Native Americans communicated with one another. Inform students that Native Americans primarily used oral language as a way to communicate. Stories were told by a storyteller or another person in the tribe; these stories usually depicted Native American culture, major events, and aspects of nature. Ceremonies and rituals were held in which song and dance were the tools for communication.

2. Explain to the class that tribes sometimes used a story belt as a way to mark a significant event. Totem poles and sand painting were also used to communicate with others. Borrow books from the library that discuss Native American culture, beliefs, and history. Try to find books that have illustrations or photographs.

3. Inform the class that they will be making story belts that tell of some aspect of Native American life. They may create story belts that feature the highlight of some event, such as a treaty signing or a battle. They may make a story belt that shows a common activity in the daily lives of Native Americans, such as fishing, hunting, or cooking. Another idea might be to show a ceremony or ritual.

4. To make the story belts, ask each student to choose a piece of construction paper. Have them cut the paper in half lengthwise and glue two short ends together, overlapping them slightly, to form one long strip.

5. Ask each student to sketch a scene for the belt, using pencils.

6. When the sketches have been completed, distribute different colors of yarn and other collage materials to the class. Students may glue these materials to their belts.

7. When the belts are dry, ask students to place them on tables for everyone to see. Give the children ten minutes to browse through them. When the ten minutes are up, ask students to return to their seats, and have one child at a time display his or her belt. Ask the class to guess what the symbolism on each belt means. After all the guesses, the creator of the belt may share its meaning with the class.

    Creative Projects

Background Check Graphs

Ask the class to describe their ethnic backgrounds while a volunteer records their comments on a chalkboard. When students are finished, categorize the backgrounds. Encourage students to create categories, such as continents (Europe, Africa, Asia, and so on) or hemispheres (Northern, Southern, Eastern, and Western).

Have the class work together to place the different ethnic groups under each heading. (Students of mixed heritage may choose the category they wish to be represented in.) Then ask students to make up a class circle graph showing the various categories. For example, if 6 students in a class of 24 are of Asian heritage, a category entitled "Asia" would take up 1/4 of the circle. Ask students to convert the fractions of the circle graph into percentages.

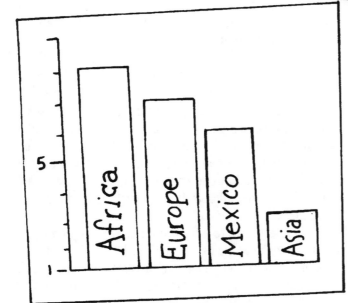

Next, ask the class to create a bar graph that shows the various categories. Students may decide whether the graph will read left to right or bottom to top. If bottom to top is chosen, write the different categories along the bottom of the paper. If desired, have volunteers make drawings representing the category next to each label.

Compare and contrast the results of the graph. Which represents the majority of the class? The smallest minority? Are any totals half of another total? A third? In what part of the world did most of the ethnic groups originate?

For extra credit, students may conduct an ethnic background survey in another class in the school, or within a group of their friends. Ask students to make up circle or bar graphs showing the results and then share them with the class.

Houses Around the World

MATERIALS:

bright-colored bulletin board paper
stapler
black permanent marker
9" x 12" different-colored construction paper
crayons and markers
scissors
thumbtacks
tape

DIRECTIONS:

1. Cover a bulletin board with brightly colored paper. Draw a grid on the board of 9" squares, with six squares in the vertical column and four squares in the horizontal column. Along the bottom and beginning on the left, write a letter of the alphabet (starting with *A*) next to each 9" section. Along the left side and beginning at the bottom, write a number (starting with *1*) next to each 9" section.

2. Distribute construction paper to the students and ask them to fold the top right corner down to the bottom of the paper, lining up the edges. Students should then cut off the excess that is not covered by the folded-down section of paper. On the square remaining, have students draw a picture of a home they find interesting. The home may be one built in their own or a different country, or it may be a futuristic home they have created.

3. Collect the drawings and shuffle them. On the back of one of the drawings, tape a picture of a piece of furniture that might be found in the home shown.

Then tack all of the homes to the board so they line up in rows and columns corresponding to the letters and numbers on the grid. Leave spaces or create another grid row if necessary.

4. To do the activity, choose two students to be the turners. Ask volunteers to name coordinates, first the letter coordinate and then the number coordinate, in order to find the piece of furniture taped to the back of one of the drawings. The turner closest to the block identified can turn it over to show the back. If no furniture picture is attached, the drawing is taken off the board, and another coordinate is called. Continue asking students to call coordinates until the furniture is found.

5. An alternative to a furniture picture is a picture of a person or the name of a home (trailer, adobe, apartment). This activity can also be played as a concentration game if two of the same pictures are taped to the backs of two home drawings.

Notable Names Gallery

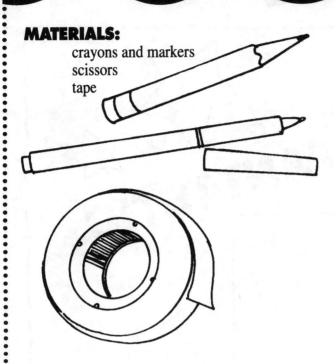

MATERIALS:

crayons and markers
scissors
tape

DIRECTIONS:

1. Reproduce the frame on page 52 once for each student. Have students color the frames and cut them out.

2. Inform students that they will be drawing a portrait or other representation of someone they feel is important to today's society, or someone who was great in his or her time. Bring students to the library to research their choices. Encourage students to discover notable names in all areas of life: sports, medicine, science, law, advocacy, education, leadership, business, government, entertainment, and the arts.

3. When students have chosen whom they wish to draw, they should draw portraits within the borders of their frames.

4. When the portraits are finished, ask each student to write a paragraph or two explaining why he or she chose the subject and how the person selected helped to enrich society.

5. Tape the portraits and paragraphs to a wall. Ask volunteers to add a border around the portrait gallery. They may decorate the border to reflect the subjects of the display, using phrases attributed to these people, comments made about them, or art symbolizing their work.

Creative Projects

Well Done

FANTASTIC

SUPERB

Good Work

WONDERFUL

Creative Projects

Video Portraits

To help encourage students to learn more about great artists throughout history, have them create video "portraits" of selected artists. Begin by providing a list of artists from which students may choose. (Each student should select a different artist.) Some suggestions are:

Leonardo da Vinci   Michelangelo
Vincent van Gogh   Grandma Moses
Norman Rockwell   Mary Cassatt
Pablo Picasso   Edgar Degas
Claude Monet   Marc Chagall
David Hockney   Georgia O'Keeffe

Give each child plenty of time to research his or her artist. Encourage students to read biographies, encyclopedia articles, and art books about their subjects. Students may also wish to contact museums that might have more information available.

Remind students to research the time period in which

the artist lived. Students should be aware of the types of dress, foods, homes, entertainment, and other aspects of life known to their subjects.

When the research has been completed, have students compose a short speech in their artist's voice, telling about his or her life. Help students practice their speeches, making sure they are brief, interesting, and accurate.

Ask each student to prepare a costume resembling clothes that his or her artist might have worn. If desired, students may be allowed to use makeup to heighten the effect.

Videotape each speech as it is performed. Allow students time to critique their performances.

Let students take turns bringing the videotape home to share with their families.

53

Puzzle Pieces File-Folder Game

MATERIALS:

- crayons or markers
- scissors
- glue
- letter-sized file folder
- oaktag
- four different-colored pieces of oaktag
- large envelope
- number cube, or die

DIRECTIONS:

1. Reproduce the game board on pages 55-56 once. Color the game board, cut it out, and mount it on the inside of a letter-sized file folder.

2. Reproduce the game cards on page 57 five times. Color the game cards, mount them on oaktag, and cut them out.

3. Reproduce the blank puzzle on page 58 once for each player. Mount the blank puzzles on oaktag.

4. Cut a 1" square from each of four different-colored pieces of oaktag to use as playing pieces.

5. Reproduce the "How to Play" instructions on this page once. Glue the instructions to the front of the file folder.

6. Write a question on each game card dealing with a subject that is currently being studied in class. For example, if the class has been learning about ancient Greece, you may wish to ask students to identify Greek letters, give the date of the Greco-Roman War, or name the capital city of ancient Greece.

7. Store the game board, playing cards, playing pieces, and a number cube in an envelope. Glue the envelope to the back of the file folder.

HOW TO PLAY:

(for two to four players)

1. Each player draws an original picture on a blank jigsaw puzzle. Players should ask their teacher if the pictures should be about a specific class subject or about anything they wish. Players should make sure that their drawings touch every puzzle piece and then carefully cut the pieces apart.

2. Each player should place his or her puzzle pieces in a separate pile next to the game board.

3. Players place their playing pieces on "Start" and place the game cards facedown in a pile in the center of the game board. Players then roll the number cube. The player who rolls the highest number goes first.

4. The first player rolls the number cube and moves his or her piece the appropriate number of spaces along the game board. If the player lands on a space that has a star, he or she may draw a game card from the pile. If the player answers the question on the card correctly, he or she may take one puzzle piece from his or her pile. If the question is not answered correctly, the next player goes. Players should try to fit their puzzle pieces together as they gain pieces by answering questions.

5. Play continues clockwise around the game board. The first player to collect all of his or her puzzle pieces and complete the puzzle is the winner.

54

© 1996 Troll Creative Teacher Ideas

Creative Projects

Puzzle Pieces File-Folder Game

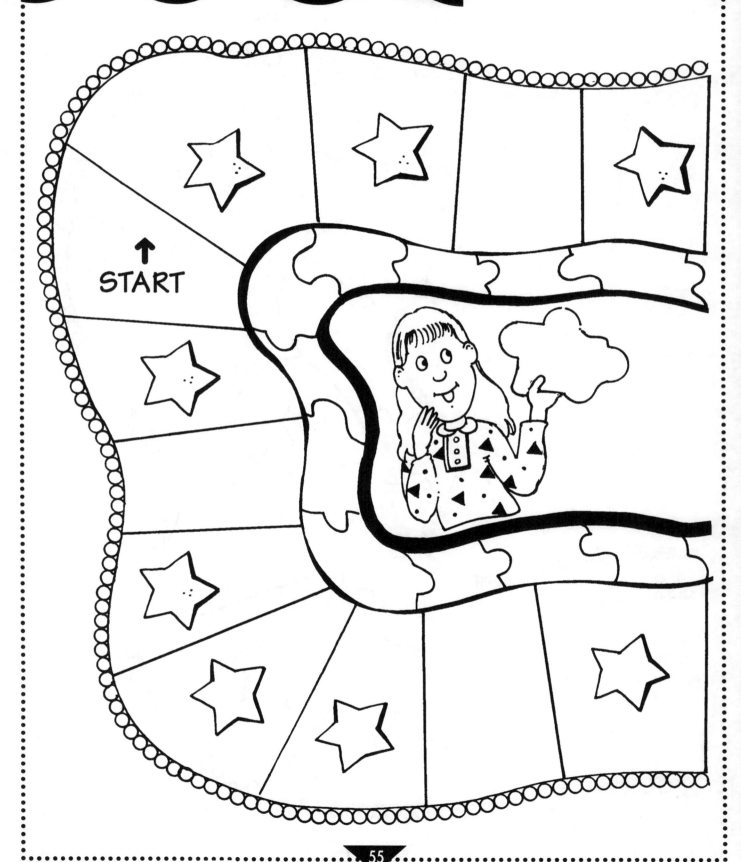

START

Creative Projects

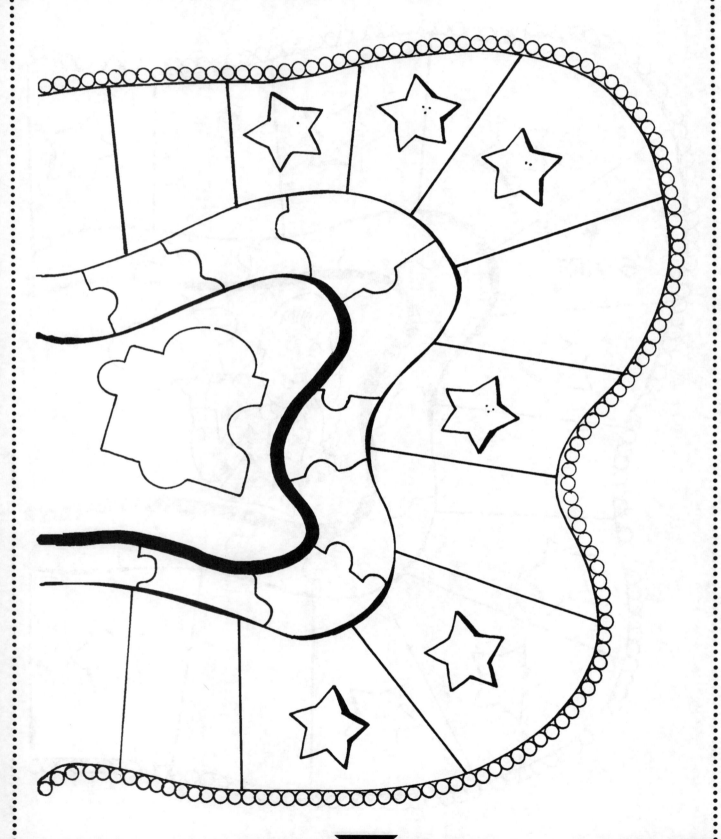

Puzzle Pieces File-Folder Game

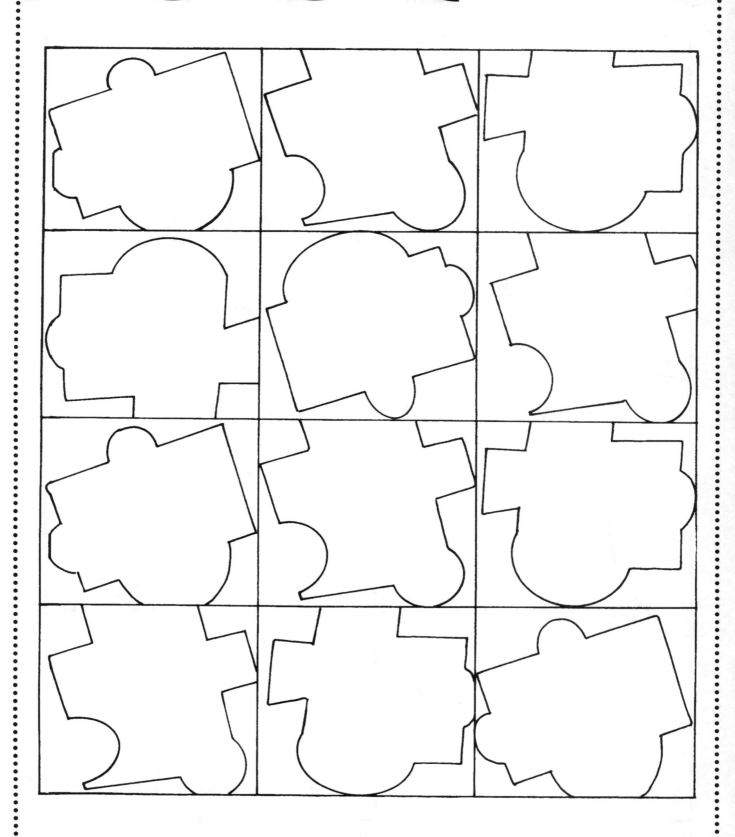

Creative Projects

Puzzle Pieces File-Folder Game

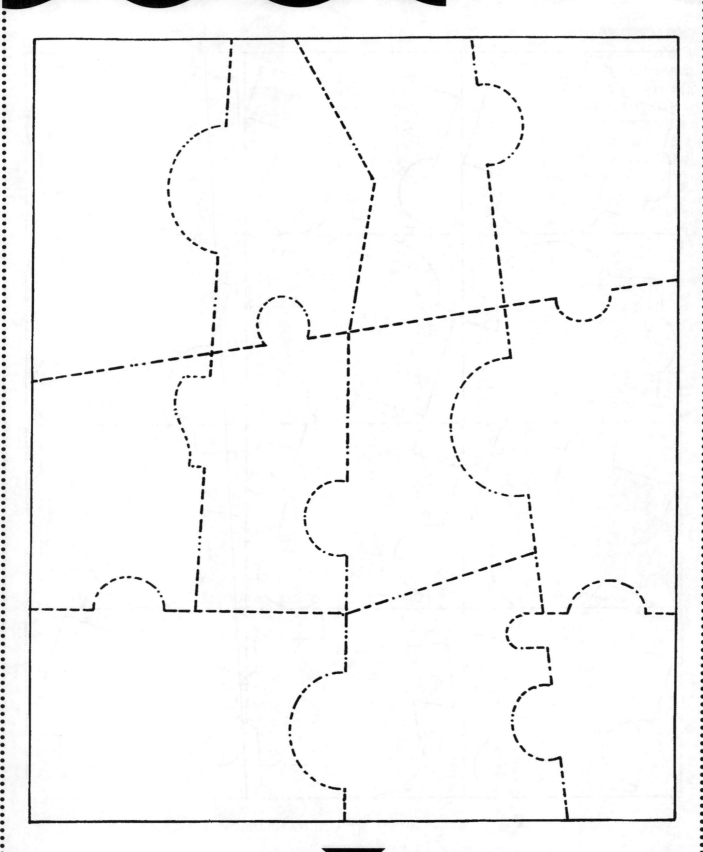

Creative Projects

Younger Buddies

DIRECTIONS:

1. Match the class up with a kindergarten class (in the same school, if possible). Assign a different kindergartner to each student.

2. Tell students that they are going to be biographers for the younger children. Explain that the biographies will be presented to the kindergartners in small booklets, which the students will make for their younger buddies. Ask each student to prepare a list of questions to ask each kindergartner. Some suggested questions are:

> How many people are in your family?
>   Tell me about them.
> What are the names of your friends?
> When is your birthday?
> Where were you born?
> What are your hobbies?
> What are your favorite sports or games?
> What is your favorite part of school?
> Have you ever taken a trip? Where to?
> What have you learned in kindergarten?
> What do you want to be when you grow up?

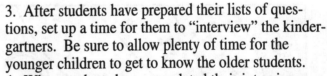

3. After students have prepared their lists of questions, set up a time for them to "interview" the kindergartners. Be sure to allow plenty of time for the younger children to get to know the older students.

4. When students have completed their interviews, have them return to the classroom to work on the biography booklets. Provide students with 7" x 12" colored oaktag, crayons or markers, old magazines and catalogs, and any other desired materials to use to make their booklets.

5. Have students fold the pieces of oaktag in half to make pages for their biographies. Each student may put as many pages in the biography booklet as he or she wants. For example, one page might say, "Chris was born on April 15, 1990. He lives with his mother and father and baby brother. He has one dog." A student may wish to draw pictures of the kindergartner's family or cut out pictures to illustrate the text.

6. Review the biographies with the students before presenting them to the kindergartners. Allow time for each student to read the biography to his or her kindergarten buddy.

59

All About Ben

Help the class put on a puppet show about Benjamin Franklin's life. Divide the class into several groups: researchers, writers, and backstage crew.

Allow the researchers time to go the school library to gather information about Benjamin Franklin. Encourage students to take plenty of notes, either on lined paper or index cards. Researchers should find out about Franklin's home life, things that happened to him when he was growing up, his involvement with newspapers, his contributions to the Declaration of Independence, his wife and children, his inventions, his time in France, and other important information about his life.

Have the researchers work with the writers to outline the play. Give the writers plenty of time to create dialogue and narration.

After reviewing the script for the play and revising it as necessary, ask volunteers to keyboard the script on a computer. Distribute copies to the class.

Reproduce the figures on page 61–65 once. Have volunteers color the figures, mount them on oaktag, and cut them out.

Glue a long craft stick to the bottom of each figure.

Have the backstage crew create any other figures that are depicted in the play, as well as the necessary props and backgrounds (for example, a kite, a Franklin stove, a library, the University of Pennsylvania, a city hospital, etc.). Provide the backstage crew with a puppet stage, or help them make one using a large cardboard box, paints, and fabric for curtains.

Choose students to manipulate the puppets and be the voice of Benjamin Franklin at the different stages of his life. Choose other students to do the same for the other characters in the play. Choose one student to be the narrator throughout the play.

After the play has been rehearsed to everyone's satisfaction, invite a class from one of the younger grades to come in and see the show. If desired, videotape the performance and allow students to take turns bringing the videotape home to share with their families.

Creative Projects

All About Ben

Ben
6 years

Ben
14 years

Creative Projects

Ben
Franklin

Creative Projects

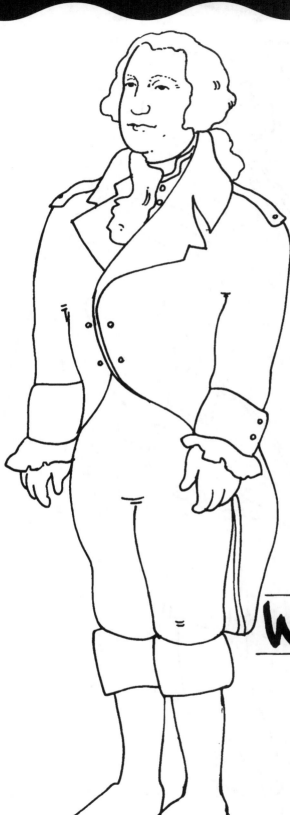

Washington

Louis
XVI

Marie
Antoinette

Inventive Inventions

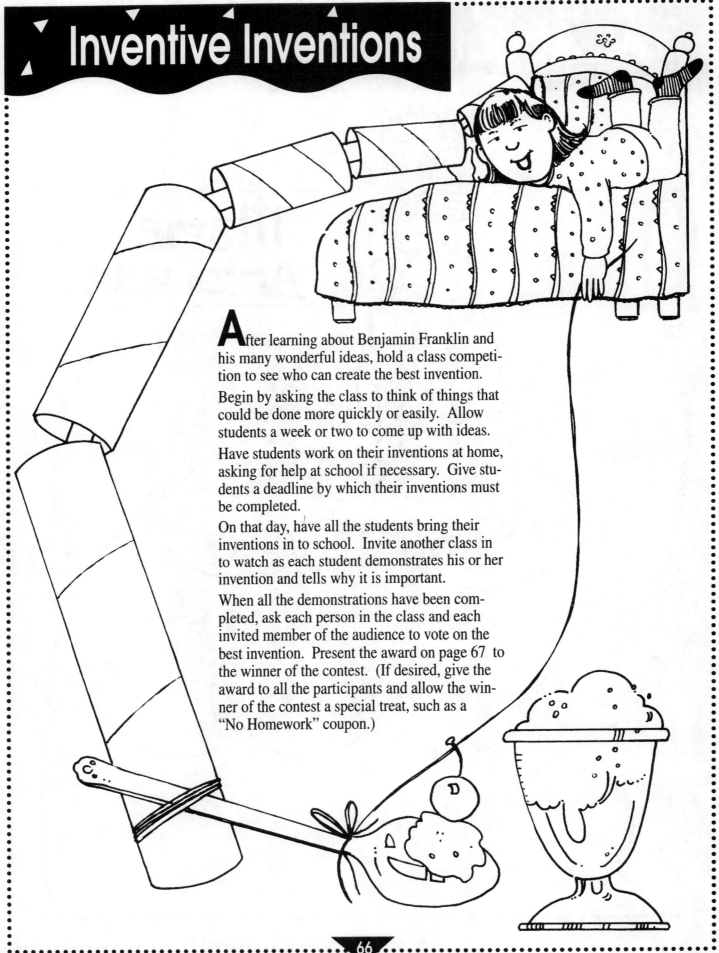

After learning about Benjamin Franklin and his many wonderful ideas, hold a class competition to see who can create the best invention.

Begin by asking the class to think of things that could be done more quickly or easily. Allow students a week or two to come up with ideas.

Have students work on their inventions at home, asking for help at school if necessary. Give students a deadline by which their inventions must be completed.

On that day, have all the students bring their inventions in to school. Invite another class in to watch as each student demonstrates his or her invention and tells why it is important.

When all the demonstrations have been completed, ask each person in the class and each invited member of the audience to vote on the best invention. Present the award on page 67 to the winner of the contest. (If desired, give the award to all the participants and allow the winner of the contest a special treat, such as a "No Homework" coupon.)

Most wonderful invention!

Presented to _____

on _____

for creating the innovative invention

_____

_____

Presented by: _____

Message in the Bottle

MATERIALS:

plastic bottles of various shapes and sizes
old magazines
glue
colored yarn
clear polyurethane and brushes

DIRECTIONS:

1. Ask the class to bring in a medium- to large-sized plastic bottle. Inform the students that they will be decorating the bottles according to themes of their choice. Some suggested themes are: fashion, school, family, friends, music, sports, and cars.

2. Once a student chooses a theme, he or she may begin cutting pictures from magazines. The pictures should reflect the theme chosen. Words that describe or define the chosen themes may also be cut out. Or students may wish to cut out letters that can be glued together to form words. When students think they have collected enough materials to cover their bottles, they may begin gluing on the pictures and words.

3. Every part of the bottle should be covered except the neck and handle (if there is one). These areas can be covered by coating them with glue and wrapping colored yarn around them until they are completely covered.

4. After all the materials have been glued onto each bottle, cover the bottles with a coat of clear polyurethane. This will preserve the pictures and keep them from tearing.

5. Have students place their bottles on their desks and then browse among the bottles. Ask them to guess the theme of each bottle and check their guesses with the creators of the bottles.

Thread Designs

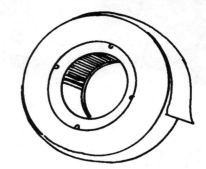

MATERIALS:

large sheets of colored oaktag   scissors
blunt needles   different-colored thread
tape

DIRECTIONS:

1. Distribute oaktag and scissors to the class. Ask each student to cut a 5" x 5" square.
2. Demonstrate how to use a needle to poke holes along opposite or perpendicular edges of a square. The number of holes on each side should be equal.
3. Ask students to choose a thread color and then show them how to thread their needles. The thread should be a single strand; do not double it. Leave about 4" hanging from the other side of the eye of the needle. Knot the end on the longer strand.
4. Show students how to insert the needle from the back of the oaktag, beginning at the first hole on one side. Have them gently pull on the thread until all the thread is through and they feel the knot catch. Then have them tape the knot in place on the back of the oaktag.
5. Students then push the needle through the last hole along the other edge, front to back, and then insert the needle into the second hole on the beginning edge (back to front) and into the second-to-last hole in the other edge (front to back).
6. Students should continue the process until the last hole is reached. The thread should overlap along the middle holes. Cut off the excess thread and tape the remaining 1" to the back of the oaktag. Display the thread pictures on the wall.
7. If a student would like to make another thread picture, encourage him or her to try something more difficult. A student might first like to draw a picture on the oaktag that contains a square or triangular shape, such as a sailboat, and then do the threading on just the sail. The rest of the picture may be colored in with crayons or markers.

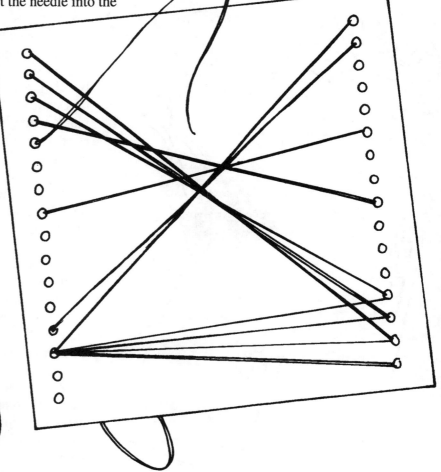

Creative Projects

Notepaper Gifts

MATERIALS:

craft sticks	paints and paintbrushes
glue	clear polyurethane
collage materials	white paper
scissors	potatoes
plastic knives	jar and container lids
small sponges	large-sized clipboard clips

DIRECTIONS:

1. Demonstrate to the class how to make a clipboard by lining up eight craft sticks, side by side. To hold them together, squeeze a line of glue along a ninth stick and press it to the row of sticks, about 1" below their tops, as shown. Repeat, using a tenth stick 1" from the bottom of the row.

2. Have students paint the clipboards. When the paint has dried, students can then apply a coat of clear polyurethane. This will help prevent the paint from cracking and strengthen the clipboards. When dry, the clipboards may be decorated with collage materials around the edges.

3. Ask students to cut about 20 sheets of white paper so their size is 1" smaller all around than the clipboard. Lay these aside.

4. Demonstrate to the class how to cut a shape into a potato to use in printmaking: Cut a potato in half, rinse it, and dry it. Using a knife, cut a shape into the center of the cut side, going down about 1", as shown. When the shape is finished, sink the knife into the side of the potato, about 1" down from the cut side, and pull it around the edges of the shape. Do not cut into the shape, or it will fall off.

5. Encourage students to create abstract designs on their potatoes. Remind them that the shapes will be used to make a border or design on their notepaper, so they must be fairly small.

6. Cut sponges to fit into the jar lids. Pour a small amount of paint over the sponges. To make the prints on their notepaper, students will press their potatoes into a sponge, then press them gently onto their papers.

7. When students have finished decorating their notepaper, show them how to clip the paper onto the center top of the clipboard, using a large-sized clip. Students may wish to wrap their clipboards and paper with tissue paper and decorate them with ribbon before presenting them as gifts.

Abstract Designs

MATERIALS:

oaktag
scissors
white easel paper or large sheets
   of butcher paper
jar lids
sponges
paints

DIRECTIONS:

1. Distribute oaktag scraps and scissors to the class. Ask students to cut shapes and designs from the oaktag.

2. When each student has cut one or more shapes, have him or her place a piece of white paper or butcher paper on the table. Then ask each child to place his or her shape onto the paper.

3. Pour small amounts of paint into jar lids, encouraging the students to decide which colors to use. Use flexible sponges to dip into the paints. Demonstrate how to dip a corner into the paint and then, holding the oaktag design with one hand and the sponge with the other, rub the sponge from the center of the design out onto the paper. Continue until the design has been completely outlined.

4. Encourage students to repeat the process over their entire papers. If an oaktag design becomes too weak or another color is desired, students may cut a new design from oaktag to replace the original one.

5. Tape the abstracts onto a wall or bulletin board. Overlap the edges of the papers slightly so the display resembles a wall mural.

Paint Toss

MATERIALS:

old newspapers
tape
butcher paper
paints and paint cups
string
scissors

DIRECTIONS:

1. Ask a group of four students to cover a large area on a wall, either indoors or outside, by taping old newspapers to the wall. The wall should be completely covered, and the floor under the wall area chosen should be covered, as well. Tape a large sheet of white paper or butcher paper onto the center of this covered space.

2. Pour small amounts of paints into paint cups. If desired, use appropriate seasonal colors. Choose a group of students to paint first. Ask each of these students to cut a length of string.

3. Demonstrate how to lower the string into a paint cup, swish it around until it is covered with paint, then raise it above the cup. Using the first finger and thumb, gently slide them down the length of the string so excess paint will fall into the paint cup.

4. Standing about 3' from the butcher paper, have students throw their strings at the paper. They must toss the strings underhanded. The strings may be balled up or left loose in the palm before tossing.

5. When the first group of students is done tossing, compare their string impressions. What shape does balled-up string make? What shape does loose string create? Does having a shorter string or a longer string make a difference? How?

6. Continue paint tossing until everyone has had a turn and the paper is well decorated. Tape the mural to a wall where all may admire their work.

Creative Projects

Molded Candles

MATERIALS:

pint milk containers
scissors
pencils
string
small washers
paraffin
old crayons
two cans, one smaller than the other
water
hot plate
sticks

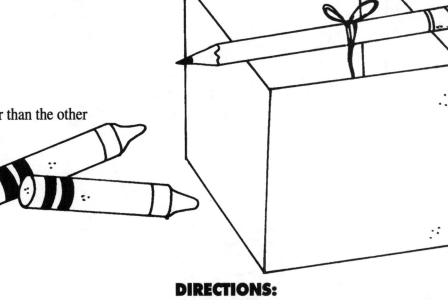

DIRECTIONS:

1. Collect containers, then wash and dry them. Show students how to cut off the tops of their containers and down the sides until the containers are square.

2. Have students measure the lengths of their containers from top to bottom and then cut lengths of string 2" longer than their measurements.

3. Have students tie one end of the string around the center of a pencil and tie the other end to a small washer. They should then place the pencil across the open tops of the containers so the strings hang down the centers.

4. Place a small can inside a large can and add water to the larger can until it comes about halfway up the side of the small can. Place the cans on a hot plate and turn it on high. Place a piece of paraffin in the small can.

5. Unwrap the crayons. Place the crayons in with the paraffin, using one color at a time.

6. When the paraffin and crayons begin to melt, stir them until well blended. Carefully pour the paraffin into the student's mold until 3/4 full. Let cool and harden.

7. Containers can be removed by gently ripping them down the sides or by kneading them gently until the candle loosens from the sides.

8. As an added touch for holidays or gifts, candles may be placed on small pie tins and decorated with collage materials glued around the candle base.

Creative Projects

Sand-sational Pictures

MATERIALS:

9" x 12" white construction paper   pencils
glue   colored sand
small cardboard or plastic containers   scissors
large sheets of colored oaktag

DIRECTIONS:

1. Distribute a piece of white construction paper to each student. Inform the students that they will be making pictures with sand. The first step is to sketch their pictures lightly in pencil.
2. Pour a different color sand into each small cardboard or plastic container. Lay the containers out on the students' work surface, along with glue.
3. Demonstrate to the class how to squeeze a line of glue along the pencil marks on their pictures and then sprinkle sand onto the glue lines. Explain that if they do a small area at a time, then shake the excess sand off, it will be easier.
4. Students may just outline different objects in their pictures with sand or smooth glue in each area and completely cover the pictures.
5. When their pictures are dry, have students choose a color of oaktag that will complement the colors in their sand pictures. They should cut the oaktag about 1" larger all around than their pictures, and then glue the pictures onto the oaktag backing.
6. Hang the pictures on a bulletin board or other display area. Pictures may be made based on the seasons, holidays, or themes on which students are currently working.

     Creative Projects

Fantastic Foil Art

MATERIALS:

small objects
foil
scissors
12" x 18" colored construction paper
glue

DIRECTIONS:

1. Collect small objects from around the class-room or ask students to bring in objects from home to use to make foil impressions. Objects that will work well are those that are not too thick and not too sharp.

2. Students may cut foil pieces that are slightly larger than the objects they wish to use, or a large sheet of foil can be cut and different impressions made all over it. Students may use the objects they brought in or borrow those brought in by others.

3. Show students how to lay their objects on a flat surface and then place the foil over them. Using a very light touch, they should rub the foil from the center out. An impression of the object should work into the foil. For example, if leaves are being used, the leaf should be placed on a table and the foil over it. Starting at the center of the leaf, a student should run a finger over the foil and continue all around the leaf. The veins and leaf outline should appear on the foil.

4. Students who have used small pieces of foil may wish to cut around the outlines of the impressions they make. They may arrange them on a piece of construction paper and glue each one down. Students who have done many impressions on a large piece of foil may glue around its edges and between impressions and press the foil onto a piece of construction paper.

5. Display the foil impressions on a bulletin board under the title "Foiled Again!" Ask students to guess what objects were used for each impression.

Creative Projects

Mood Painting

MATERIALS:

watercolor paints and thin brushes
cups
9" x 12" white construction paper
scraps of different-colored construction paper
scissors
glue

DIRECTIONS:

1. Distribute watercolor paints and brushes to pairs of students. Ask one child from each pair to fill a cup 3/4 full with water. Have the other partner bring two pieces of white paper to their work spaces.

2. Inform the class that they will be creating backgrounds for a picture they will make on the paper when the paints dry. To make the background, students will dip their brushes several times in water and tickle the paint color they have chosen to use first. Tell students that they must get the brushes quite wet.

3. After getting color on their brushes, students can use them on their papers. Encourage students to experiment with different strokes and techniques. They may want to make lines or swirls, color in whole areas, dot the paper, or create spirals along the length of the paper.

4. Remind students that when they want to change colors, they should rinse their brushes in the water cup. After each new color or technique, ask students to hold up their papers and slant them up and down. This will run the colors into one another, creating new designs and colors.

5. When the paints have dried, ask students to look at their paintings and try to choose moods that correspond with them. Then ask them to use colored construction paper to create foreground pictures that will fit in with the moods of their paintings.

6. Students may wish to rip their papers to create the foregrounds or they may use scissors for a cleaner look. For example, if a student feels his or her picture is reminiscent of a dark, creepy night, he or she may want to rip the paper in order to make the foreground picture seem distorted and eerie.

7. After the pictures are done, ask each student to write a paragraph describing his or her scene. Encourage the students to show their paintings and read their paragraphs to the class.

Creative Projects

Classroom Calligraphy

MATERIALS:

photocopier paper
calligraphy pens
black ink

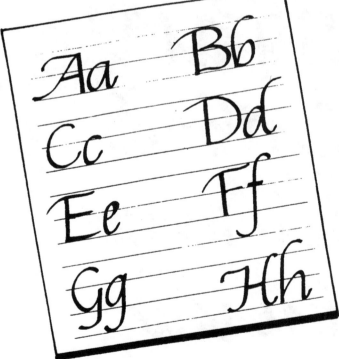

DIRECTIONS:

1. Have a class discussion about the art of calligraphy. Ask if anyone knows what calligraphy is, and if anyone has ever tried to write using calligraphy.

2. Explain to students that calligraphy is a form of decorative handwriting that was developed by the Chinese over 2,000 years ago. To create their work, calligraphers usually use a special type of pen that is dipped into ink.

3. Distribute white photocopier paper to students. Provide a calligraphy pen for every three or four students, as well as a bottle of black ink. During free time, students should be encouraged to experiment on the white paper with the calligraphy pen and ink, discovering the various thicknesses of lines that can be drawn. Ask students to write their names and addresses, or the alphabet.

4. When the class has become more comfortable using the calligraphy pens, reproduce the reference sheet on page 78 and the worksheets on pages 79–81 once for each student. Ask students to practice writing calligraphy letters.

5. If desired, give students additional copies of the worksheets and more time to practice their calligraphy. When students have become proficient calligraphers, ask a group of volunteers to make a calligraphy alphabet border for the classroom.

Creative Projects

Name _____

Formal Italic

ABCDEFG
HIJKLMN
OPQRSTUV
WXYZabcd
efghijklmn
opqrstuvw
xyz

Calligraphy Alphabet

Name _____

Aa

Bb

Cc

Dd

Ee

Ff

Gg

Hh

Calligraphy Alphabet

Name _____

Ii

Jj

Kk

Ll

Mm

Nn

Oo

Pp

Calligraphy Alphabet

Name _____

Qq

Rr

Ss

Tt

Uu

Vv   *Ww*

Xx   *Yy*

Zz

Fancy Folding

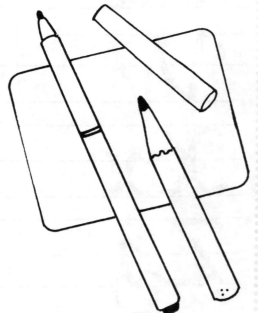

MATERIALS:

scissors
glue
paints and paintbrushes
decorating materials (tissue paper, pipe cleaners, buttons, etc.)

DIRECTIONS:

1. Reproduce the geometric figures on pages 83–86 several times for each student. Have students cut out the figures.
2. Show students how to fold each figure together into a 3-D shape by folding along the dotted lines.
3. Glue the appropriate tabs in place to complete each figure.
4. Ask students to glue their shapes together to make a new shape or to represent something, such as a home, a car, or a creature from outer space.
5. Provide students with paints and paintbrushes to use to decorate their creations. You may also wish to let them use tissue paper, pipe cleaners, buttons, and other decorating materials.

Fancy Folding

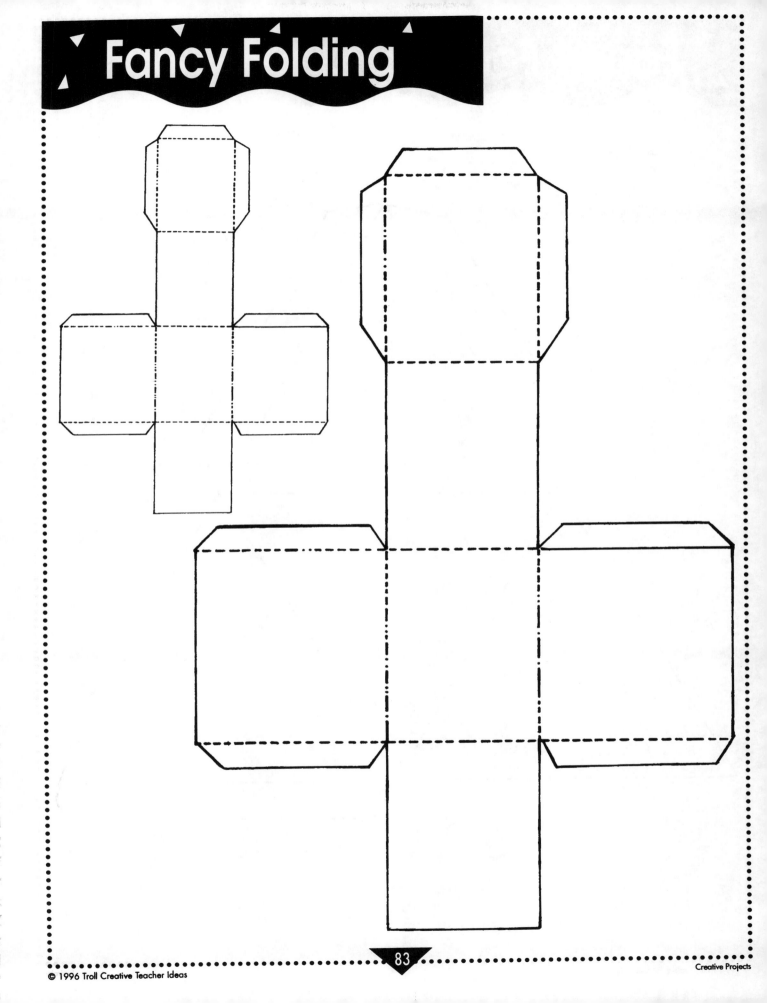

Creative Projects

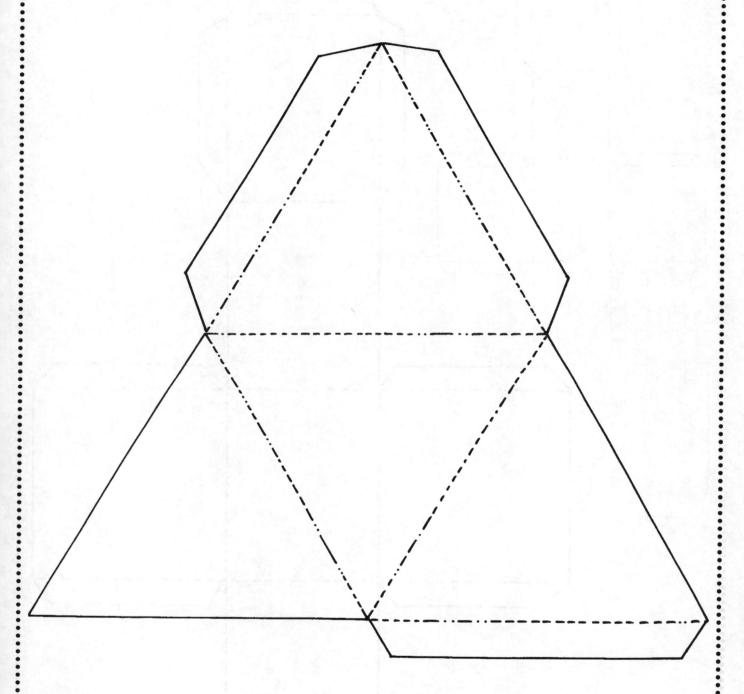

Fancy Folding

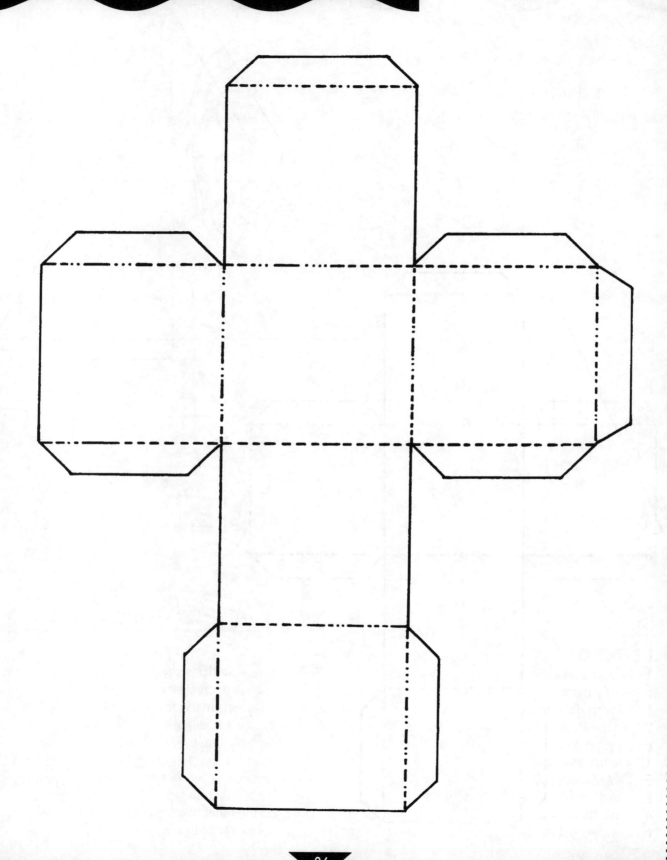

Creative Projects

What a Relief!

MATERIALS:

large pieces of cardboard (approximately 12" x 18")
flour and water
small bowls
old newspapers
paints and paintbrushes

DIRECTIONS:

1. Inform students that they are going to create relief maps of a particular area they have been studying. Divide the class into pairs.
2. Assign a country or region to each pair. Give each pair a large piece of cardboard (approximately 12" x 18") to use as a base.
3. Show students how to mix flour and water together in a small bowl until it forms a thin, sticky mixture.
4. Have students dip strips of newspaper into the mixture, wiping off the excess between their thumbs and forefingers. Students should then lay the newspaper onto the base to create the terrain for their relief maps.
5. Tell students to use the newspaper strips to make mountain ranges and hills. When each pair is satisfied with their relief map, place the maps aside to dry.
6. Provide students with paints and paintbrushes to use to indicate grassy plains, mountains, deserts, water, etc. Ask each pair to label their map clearly.
7. Place the relief maps on flat surfaces around the room for everyone to see.

Creative Projects

Thank-You Graffiti

MATERIALS:

mural paper
old newspapers
paints and paintbrushes
markers

DIRECTIONS:

1. To make an original thank-you note for classroom visitors, school workers, field trip speakers, or other class benefactors, begin by laying out a large piece of mural paper on the classroom floor.

2. Place newspapers under the edges of the mural paper all around.

3. Provide students with paints and paintbrushes. Have students paint a red brick pattern onto the mural paper, to resemble a wall.

4. When the paint has dried, have a group of students paint a message across the top of the mural (for example, "Thank You, Ms. Doherty!"). Then let each student write a personal thank-you message and sign his or her name. Students may use paints or markers to write their messages.

5. Prepare the thank-you note for delivery by carefully rolling up the mural and then tying it with a festive ribbon.

Creative Projects

Burlap Wall Hangings

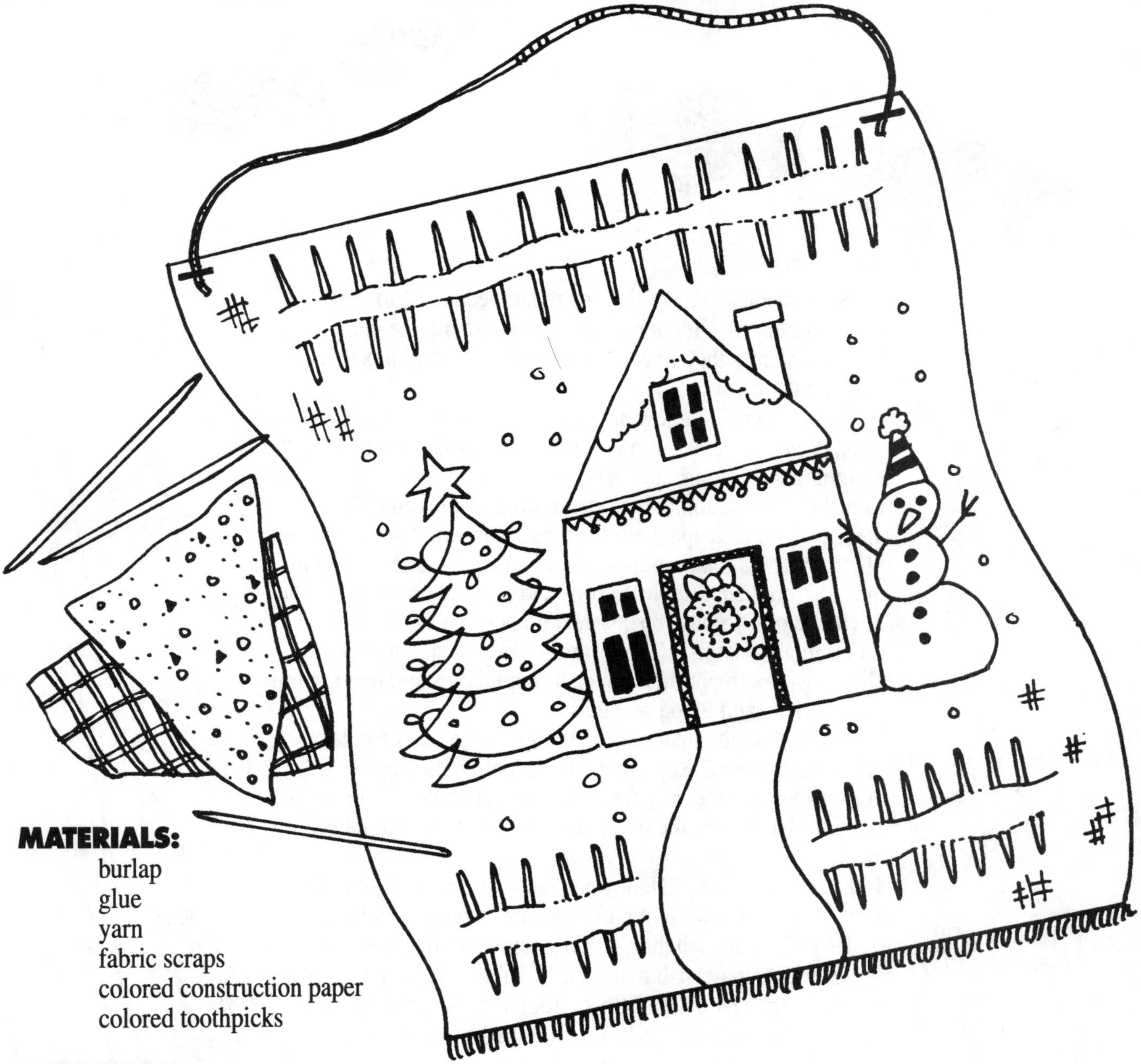

MATERIALS:
- burlap
- glue
- yarn
- fabric scraps
- colored construction paper
- colored toothpicks

DIRECTIONS:

1. To decorate the classroom for holidays and other special occasions, have the class make burlap wall hangings. Begin by distributing a length of burlap to each student.

2. Tell students to sketch the designs for their wall hangings on paper. When they are satisfied, have them transfer the designs onto the burlap.

3. Provide students with yarn, which may be glued to the burlap to form the outlines of figures and shapes. Show students how to cut and glue fabric scraps or colored construction paper to fit inside the figures and shapes on their wall hangings.

4. Students may also weave colored toothpicks in and out of the burlap to add color to their wall hangings.

5. Staple one end of a length of yarn to the top right and the other end to the top left corner of each wall hanging. Attach the wall hangings around the classroom using thumbtacks or pushpins. If desired, let the children bring their wall hangings home to decorate their own rooms.

Haunted House Fun

DIRECTIONS:

1. Have students create their own haunted house to entertain younger classes. Begin by brainstorming with the class about haunted houses they have visited. Ask what features they enjoyed the most.

2. List students' suggestions and comments on the chalkboard. Then divide the class into groups of four or five students each, assigning to each group a list of materials to acquire and props to make. For example, if students suggest a creepy "feely" area, with cooked spaghetti for brains and squashed grapes for blood and guts, one group would be in charge of bringing in the cold, cooked pasta in a bowl, and another group would be in charge of bringing in squashed grapes in a bowl. A third group might design the prop for the feely area, which would allow visitors to put their hands through holes and feel the imitation brains and blood and guts.

3. Ask that all the materials be brought in to class the day before Halloween. Reproduce the invitation on page 91 as many times as necessary for each younger student to be invited. Have students color the invitations, fill them in, and deliver them.

4. Let students spend Halloween morning setting up the classroom, using colored light bulbs for dim lighting, and hanging spider webs, bats, witches, goblins, and other decorating materials. Students may wish to use desks, tables, and chairs to make a path for the visitors to follow through the haunted house.

5. After the invited class has toured the haunted house, invite them to stay for a joint Halloween party.

Creative Projects

For a hauntingly good time,
_____
come to _____
at _____ o'clock
on _____

Creative Projects

Target Practice

MATERIALS:

large sheets of oaktag
crayons and markers
scissors
bean bags

DIRECTIONS:

1. Ask the class to divide into groups of two or three. Inform them that they will be creating targets for a throwing activity. Give each group a large sheet of oaktag, crayons or markers, and scissors.

2. Allow time for the groups to decide on what type of target they should make. The targets may be made around a theme, such as the circus, a car racetrack, or a basketball game. Targets should have at least three holes in them. The holes may be the same size, or some may be larger and some smaller. If the holes are cut to different sizes, the group should assign a number to each hole depending on how difficult it is to get a bean bag through them.

3. Each group should create rules for using their target. The rules should be written clearly for others to read on the target itself or on an attached piece of paper. For example, one group may make their holes all the same size but assign a different score to each one based on the distance from the throw line to the target. Another group may assign higher scores for fancy throws, such as under a leg or over a shoulder.

4. Set the targets up around the room or gym. Targets may be propped up by chairs or low tables, or a student in the group may hold them. Give each student a bean bag and encourage him or her to try out each target. When a student is finished throwing at one target, he or she may move on to the next one.

5. Students should try out every target. When everyone has had a turn, ask the groups to share the process they went through making their targets. Encourage them to critique their work. See if anyone has suggestions for making their own or another group's target more challenging. If desired, targets may be donated to the physical education department.

Creative Projects

Be Good to Yourself!

MATERIALS:

bulletin board paper
stapler
crayons or markers
9" x 12" construction paper
scissors
glue

DIRECTIONS:

1. Inform the class that they will be creating posters that encourage students to take care of their bodies and to make healthful choices for themselves.
2. The posters may be drawings or cutouts glued to a piece of paper. They may be funny or serious. Students may use role models, such as sports figures and fitness experts, or make up their own slogans. For example, a basketball star may be drawn with a speech balloon next to him that reads, "Slam dunk drugs!" Students may wish to draw a famous person and make up a slogan for him or her to say. A student may create just a picture that symbolizes the topic, or just write a slogan and decorate the poster in eye-catching colors. Encourage students to share their work with the class.
3. Cover a bulletin board with brightly colored paper and arrange students' work on it. Ask volunteers to create a border for the board. Students may choose to write words that convey a healthy attitude, or they may draw pictures that emphasize good health. A suggested title for the bulletin board is "Be Good to Yourself!"

Creative Projects

Walking Stilts

MATERIALS:

coffee cans
nail and hammer
strong string
scissors
stickers, collage materials
glue

DIRECTIONS:

1. Ask students to bring in two coffee cans each. Have students wash out their cans and dry them.
2. Demonstrate how to punch holes about 1" up from the bottom of the cans, using a thick 3" nail and a hammer. Lay the can on its side and ask a student to hold it steady. Hold the nail on the point where the hole will be. Very firmly, hammer the nail into the can. Repeat on the opposite side. Then have the class divide into partners and punch holes in their cans.

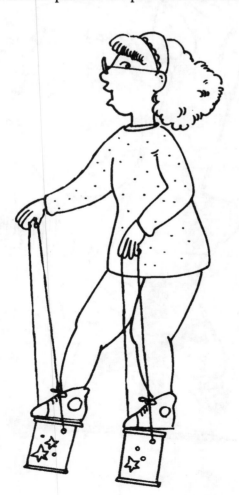

3. Still in pairs, students should measure out two lengths of string, one for each stilt. To do this, one student stands on his or her cans with arms down. The partner holds the free end of a ball of string by one of the holes in one can, then passes the ball up to the student standing on the cans. He or she then holds the string and passes the ball back to the first student. This student cuts the string a few inches longer than where it ends at the opposite hole on the can.
4. To make the string for the other stilt, the students can lay the first string out on the floor and cut the same length from the ball of string. They then repeat the process for the other partner's stilts. Students may wish to decorate their stilts with stickers and collage materials.
5. Knot the ends of the lengths of string into each hole in the cans. To walk, students will stand on their cans, holding the top of the string where it forms a loop. They must keep the string taut in order to keep the cans from falling away from their feet as they walk. For the first round of walking, ask students to walk as they would normally. Then see who can walk backwards or sideways. Encourage students to experiment safely with their stilts.

Creative Projects

Creative Thinker Award

Presented to

_____

on

_____

Presented by

Awards

Creative Projects